Rooted

In
The Storm

A 61-Day Devotional of Faith
by Beth Armstrong

Crowder-Neon Steeple "Come As you Are" 2014
℗ 2014 sixstepsrecords/Sparrow Records

Jeremy Camp-I Will Follow "Be Still" 2015
℗2015 Stolen Pride Records/Sparrow Records/Capital
Christian Music Group

Priscilla Shirer Discerning the Voice of God: How to
Recognize When God Speaks, ©2007 Moody Publishers

For Chris, Hunter, and Ella. May we forever remain rooted in Christ.

A special thank you to Mindy Armour & Kelley Hartnett. Without your help, <u>Rooted in the Storm</u> would never have made it beyond my laptop.

Dedication:

This book is dedicated to our God, who has brought my family through the most difficult storm we have faced yet. We doubted, battled fear after fear and shed many tears. Yet through it all, God—as our anchor in the storm—faithfully remained. I am thankful every day that He would use such a flawed individual in His kingdom story. While I still don't know how our story will end, I pray that the lessons God has taught me along the way will help you, too, remain anchored in whatever storm you are facing. While fears still loom, our sovereign God is faithful and has promised we will reach the shoreline together. What God has promised, He *will* see through to completion.

Introduction:

We all face storms—some we see brewing months before they hit, and others blindside us when the massive waves strike.

On Sunday, March 11, 2018, our storm made landfall as my husband, Chris, developed gall stone-induced pancreatitis and was admitted to our local hospital.

Chris's pancreatitis worsened faster than any of us realized, hurling our family into a battle for his life. When his organs began to crash unexpectedly, his physicians transferred him to another hospital 30 miles away. A few short days later, imaging showed his illness had progressed to "Acute, Infectious, Hemorrhagic, Necrotizing Pancreatitis." This new diagnosis led to an urgent transfer to the Medical Intensive Care Unit (MICU) where he was immediately sedated and intubated.

As doctors began the intubation procedure, Chris vomited, and then aspirated, the oral contrast given him a few hours earlier. His lungs rapidly filled with his own vomit, causing Acute Respiratory Distress Syndrome (ARDS). We watched helplessly as his medical team manually bagged him for more than six hours, trying to increase his oxygen levels above 40%. Chris had less than a 10% chance of surviving the day.

During these excruciating hours, I was forced to make the difficult decision to not resuscitate Chris should his heart stop. That day, our family gathered waiting to see if he would survive. Early the next morning, Chris's attending physician told me Chris was sicker than the previous day, and he warned me that I would likely need to turn off life support and let him pass peacefully. But Chris's body refused to quit.

And then the next squall hit. On March 21, 2018 at 7 a.m., less than a week after his admittance to the MICU, Chris went into cardiac arrest. I watched as his medical team performed chest compressions—trying over and over to get his heart to restart. Finally, after the longest 6 minutes of my life, it did.

Over the past 200 days, Chris's kidneys have shut down, and he's been officially diagnosed with End Stage Renal Disease. He's had a tracheotomy and continues to fight vent dependency with each breath. He's battled septic shock and more infections than I can name, including Vancomycin-Resistant Enterococci (VRE). He has burst blood vessels in his eyes that make it difficult for him to see. The medications used to keep him alive have caused critical illness peripheral neuropathy and myopathy, ravaging his muscle tissue and limiting his mobility. His internal inflammation is still so severe that we've been unable to address the stones in the common bile duct and gall bladder that caused this unending storm.

I am writing this book as I sit beside Chris's hospital bed. We've spent a month in the MICU and more than a month in the Surgical Trauma Intensive Care Unit (STICU). We've been transferred multiple times between our room at a Long-Term Acute Care facility to the STICU as Chris experiences one setback after another.

During our storm, our family has ended one school year and begun another, and we've experienced three changes of seasons. Our youngest child has celebrated her fourth birthday and started pre-kindergarten, and our oldest child has celebrated his ninth birthday and begun third grade. We've celebrated Mother's Day, Father's Day, my birthday and our 18th wedding anniversary. All without Chris by our side.

Some days, the weather seems to be clearing. More often than not, though, I'm caught off-guard as mini-squalls develop when and where I least expect them.

Still, I've found one thing to be true: *Who* and *where* I'm rooted *in* the storm determines my ability to peacefully weather each challenge, while finding hope along the way.

The daily devotions that follow are a compilation of posts I wrote during this time—each one a lesson from God. They are glimpses into the hope and grace I've experienced from the overwhelming blessings God has so graciously poured over my children and me. While my family and I may only be nearing the half-way mark for Chris's return home, we are stronger today than we have ever been because of our roots in Jesus Christ.

I pray this book will help you find peace and encouragement in your storm. More than anything, I hope you will learn that choosing to root yourself daily in Christ will change everything. He is the source of all peace, wisdom, encouragement and hope. In Him, you will find all you need.

If your storm has left you struggling with sleepless nights and a broken heart, please seek Him. Time and time again, I've realized that when I begin my day worshipping God, I have peace. When I allow distractions, hurt and unforgiveness to build walls between God and me, I struggle to find any peace or joy. Grow your roots deeper through your worship of God, and your life will bear great fruit in this season.

My sweet friend, keep going to Him with *all* that weighs on you—and leave it at His feet. He *will* carry you through this storm if you let Him.

Much Love,

Beth

"They will be like a tree planted by the water
    that sends out its roots by the stream.
It does not fear when heat comes;
    its leaves are always green.
It has no worries in a year of drought
    and never fails to bear fruit."

-Jeremiah 17:8

"Blessed is the one
    who does not walk in step with the wicked
or stand in the way that sinners take
    or sit in the company of mockers,
but whose delight is in the law of the LORD,
    and who meditates on his law day and night.
That person is like a tree planted by streams of water,
    which yields its fruit in season
and whose leaf does not wither—
    whatever they do prospers."

-Psalm 1:1-3

Day One
Eye of the Storm

As I sit in Chris's room in the MICU, listening to the ventilator pumping air for him and looking at all the monitors and IVs helping to sustain his life, I realize that we are now in the eye of the storm.

We like to convince ourselves that tomorrow we'll wake up early and have that quiet time with God. Tomorrow, we'll read our Bible and begin to work on those verses we've been meaning to memorize. We tell ourselves we'll finally make our faith a priority after we finish this last project or next month when our schedule finally calms down.

Unfortunately, the truly devastating storms often strike before our "tomorrows" have come, and we're caught unprepared. As we look around at the destruction, we wonder where God is. Maybe our life is shattered by an unexpected job loss or by the divorce papers we've feared. Maybe it's a diagnosis we can no longer deny, or a devastating betrayal finally spotlighted for all to see. Whatever the cause, eventually we all are caught in the eye of a storm.

It's what we choose to do *in* the storm that will determine our outcome. Do we choose to finally make *today* the day we prioritize our faith and walk more closely with God? Or do we allow our circumstances to push us farther out to sea?

Rooting Ourselves in Christ:

What is one thing you can do today that will help you prioritize your walk with God? How can spending time with Him today give you much-needed strength and encouragement?

_____

_____

_____

_____

_____

_____

_____

_____

_____

Day Two
God Never Wastes a Hurt

*I've received many comments about my "strength."
Each day on this journey, God has made one thing very
clear to me: My "strength," my hope and my peace are
from God. It is God who has used my life as "training" to
prepare me for this fight.*

Genesis 50:20 reminds us:

> "You intended to harm me, but God intended it
> for good to accomplish what is now being done,
> the saving of many lives."

Regardless of what the Enemy may plan, God can and
will use *every* situation for our good and His glory. God
has been expertly allowing you to walk through difficult
seasons to grow your "spiritual muscles." He has
allowed you the opportunity to witness struggles by
those closest to you so you would be better prepared
for your own difficult circumstances.

God has every intention to use this very season to draw
you closer to Him and allow you to be His light to others
as you walk through your storm. It's okay if you don't
feel strong. It's okay if you don't know what to do or
how you're going to get through this season. Focus on
today, on this hour, on this minute. Find a verse that
brings you peace and strengthens your resolve and

meditate on it. God has brought you to this season and He *will* strengthen you to endure it so His glory can grow in you and shine through you. One of my favorite verses to recite when I feel weak is Psalm 73:26: "My flesh and my heart fail; but God is the strength of my heart and my portion forever."

Rooting Ourselves in Christ

If you're struggling to see His hand at work, ask God to show you specifically how He has been equipping you to walk through this season. Ask others to pray that God strengthens you as you face this storm. How can you then use your storm to plant seeds of hope and faith in the life of another by asking God to use your storm for His glory?

_____

_____

_____

_____

_____

_____

Day Three
God Speaks Through Repetition

Because Chris developed ARDS, he must be rotated from his belly to his back and then back to his belly. It was this simple repositioning two days ago that caused his body to crash and led to more than five hours of continuous and strenuous work by the medical team to keep Chris alive and give us a fighting chance.

Before our storm hit, I encountered the theme "Fear is a Liar" for weeks. I heard Zach Williams's song play multiple times a day on the radio, and multiple daily devotionals on this topic appeared in my inbox. In fact, I began to joke with friends that I felt God wanted to make sure I very clearly understood this message—but I had no idea why since I wasn't currently walking through a season of fear. But often, that's how God works. If you pay attention, you'll see God using all kinds of resources to get your attention about a topic or message He wants to convey to you. His job is to speak; our job is to listen.

If you're not sure if God is talking to you, look for repetition of themes. Does the same song get your attention on the radio? Does a similar idea float to the surface during your quiet time? God was clearly preparing me for what was coming, and He's also preparing you.

If you are also battling fear, remember there are more than 360 verses in the Bible that address the importance of *not* being afraid. God doesn't say you won't feel fear, but He does remind us that fear is not a gift from Him. You can also find more than 360 verses in the Bible about strength—one for each day of the year.

Regardless of your season or your struggle, the Bible has a verse (or several) waiting to encourage and equip you. There is nothing you will face that God does not address in His word.

Rooting Ourselves in Christ

I promise, in the storm that you're walking through, God has a SPECIFIC message waiting for you! When you reflect over the last few days or weeks, what theme(s) are you noticing? What do you think God may be trying to speak to you today?

_____

_____

_____

_____

_____

Day Four
Peace Which Passes All Understanding

Chris was successfully able to stay on his back for 6hrs yesterday while having dialysis. The doctors are hopeful he can handle eight hours today. We have turned off the paralytic medicine, and while he remains heavily sedated and intubated, we are watching to see how his body responds.

It may seem impossible to have peace when you don't know the outcome of your storm. But God promises it's still possible. Every day, regardless of our circumstances, we each have a choice to make. We can choose to believe that the God who spoke the universe into existence is in control, and therefore we can trust Him; or, we can choose to believe only what we can see with our physical eyes and allow the stress and worry to consume us.

Especially because we don't know what the future holds, we need to lean on the One who does. We are reminded of this in Philippians 4:6-7:

> "Do not be anxious about anything, but in every situation, by prayer and petition, with thanksgiving, present your requests to God. And the peace of God, which transcends all understanding, will guard your hearts and your minds in Christ Jesus."

It is not always easy to trust an unseen God. But I promise you, when you do, you *will* have a peace that transcends all human understanding.

Rooting Ourselves in Christ

What is keeping you from peace today? What do you need to give to God today, so you can receive His peace?

_____

- -

- -

- -

- -

- -

- -

- -

- -

- -

- -

Day Five
Offer the Gift of Prayer

While Chris remains somewhat "stable," I have felt the overwhelming weight of all that lays at my feet this morning. The kids have a huge need to have a semblance of "normal," and Chris continues to need 24/7 care as his condition is still very critical. My family has a great need for me to handle the logistics of maintaining our household for our two young children, along with managing the bills that must be paid while our family's primary breadwinner remains unconscious in the MICU.

One of the greatest blessings you can give and receive during a storm is the gift of prayer. One early morning when I needed it most, a stranger offered me this gift while standing in the women's bathroom of the MICU. Her words lifted my heart and allowed me to receive God's lovingkindness when I needed it the most.

A few short days later, I was able to follow this great woman's example and offer a gift of prayer to another. This woman was watching her daughter, Kamisha, die from a brain bleed—just like her husband had suffered several years earlier. In that moment, two hurting women came together to give our hearts and fears to God. For the next several days, this stranger and I prayed together and supported each other. What we both realized is that when we stayed connected to the source of peace through prayer, we felt peace. When we allowed the chaos of the day to interfere with our time with God, then the worry and anxiety of our situation returned.

Rooting Ourselves in Christ

I want to encourage you to intentionally look for opportunities to share the gift of prayer with someone else. Is there someone who's been on your heart? If you're not comfortable yet praying with them in person, write your prayer down and then mail it to them. I promise, this is a gift that will bless you both.

_____

_____

_____

_____

_____

_____

_____

Day Six
Your Prayers Limit Satan's Power

*We just received the latest findings of the CT scan. The doctors saw **no** evidence of infectious, hemorrhagic, or necrotic pancreatitis—**only** acute pancreatitis. One week ago, we were told that his abdomen was full of dead, necrotic sepsis bowel.*

When we watch someone else walking through a difficult time, we often comment, "I'm praying for you" and leave wishing we could "do more." Even though we claim to believe in God and profess to trust Him, how often do we minimize the very thing God tells us to do?

Jeremiah 29:12 tells us:

"Then you will call on me and come and pray to me, and I will listen to you."

Our prayers are the *most* powerful weapon we have. Our prayers can thwart the Enemy's plans, strengthen our resolve, bring peace and healing to any situation and provide wisdom when we need it. The Enemy's number one goal is to deceive us into believing our prayers aren't powerful. It's his mission to do whatever it takes to distract us and keep us from using the most effective tool we have—prayer.

When we pray, we're inviting God into our situation. We're asking for God to step in and do what only God can do. The Enemy is no fool. He knows his power over our lives is limited and directly linked to our prayerful connection to the Creator of the Universe. If he can disrupt or distract our prayer life, he can cause unadulterated havoc and destruction.

Rooting Ourselves in Christ:

What can you do to increase or improve your prayer life? Where are you feeling distracted? Could it be the Enemy at work?

_____

- -

- -

- -

- -

- -

- -

- -

Day Seven
Come as You Are

This morning while the staff was rotating Chris from his belly to his back, the vent became dislodged from his lungs, causing his heart to stop. For six long minutes, I watched as they performed CPR on his lifeless body before they found a pulse.

Each new day begins with the promise of hope and healing. While some days we are reminded acutely of the fragility of life, throughout *all* days, God remains sovereign. Life and death lay solely at His feet and His discretion alone; only God is the author and finisher of our life.

David Crowder sings:

> "All who are broken, lift up your face. Lay down your hurt. Lay down your heart. Come as you are. Earth has no sorrow heaven can't heal."

I hope you know that. We may never understand the "why" of our storm, and we may never comprehend why God has allowed us or our family to walk through this season. But whatever we are facing, we can trust God. We can trust that He has a plan and a purpose to use it for our good and His glory. All He is asking is that we come to Him.

Go to God with your hurts. Go to Him with your sorrows. Go to Him with your pain, your anger, your questions, your sorrow.

He doesn't require us to *do* anything more than come, right now, right as we are.

Rooting Ourselves in Christ

What do you need to lay at the feet of Jesus? What hurt are you holding that belongs to God?

_____

- -

- -

- -

- -

- -

- -

- -

- -

- -

Day Eight
Leaving the 99

Chris developed a pneumothorax today (collapsed right lung). Thankfully after the placement of a chest tube, his lungs mostly re-inflated. However, today is officially the end of the first seven days of ARDS. ARDS typically progresses in severity in stages—each taking approximately seven days. The longer ARDS continues unresolved, the less likely it is he will survive.

It's easy to go through our busy, chaotic lives and not look past the wind and waves that surround us to see others who are also struggling. It's easy to go about our daily routine greeting the same faces each day. But if we never leave our comfortable "99," will we ever be the light in our world that God has called us to be?

In Matthew 28: 18-20, God calls each of us to go out into our specific sphere of influence and lead others to Christ. If we never choose to leave our fellow "99," how can we reach those who are lost? Is the one who has wandered off not as valuable to God as the "99" who stayed together?

At some point in your life, you were the one lost sheep. I know I was. Even as the daughter of a Southern Baptist minister, I spent years intentionally running away from God—until I found myself completely lost without Him.

God's love is so good and so reckless that He went to great lengths to find me.

There is a great blessing waiting for you if you will trust God and lead a life that intentionally welcomes all you encounter and leads them back to Him. If you will let Him, God can use *this* storm to reach another lost sheep.

Rooting Ourselves in Christ

How has God demonstrated a "reckless" love for you? Who do you know who seems "lost"? What is something you can do today to help them find their way back to God?

_____

_____

_____

_____

_____

_____

_____

_____

Day Nine
The Gift in the Trial

This morning, Chris has an increased white blood cell count and a fever. We, unfortunately, don't yet know why. We were able to turn off his sedation and are waiting to see if/when he wakes up and what his neurological function will be when that happens. His ARDS is holding steady and not progressing further.

James 1:2-4 reminds us:

> "Consider it pure joy, my brothers and sisters, whenever you face trials of many kinds, because you know that the testing of your faith produces perseverance. Let perseverance finish its work so that you may be mature and complete, not lacking anything."

This verse has been on my heart throughout the week as a steady reminder of the *"gifts"* that can be found *in* the storms of life. If we allow God to join us in the storm and seek Him in *every* aspect of it, I have no doubt that going through our personal squall can be a gift.

During our journey, God has gifted me with a chance to see, for myself, His sovereign hand at work. God has gifted me the opportunity to watch as He lovingly brought life from death and offered me a chance to apply a lifetime's worth of Sunday School lessons to real life circumstances.

My encouragement and prayer for you is this: Whatever trial you're facing, don't run from it. Don't try to control it, and don't worry about the "what ifs." Don't "busy" or "numb" yourself in any way to lessen or prevent the pain and difficulty of the trial you're facing. See the lies of fear and anxiety being whispered to you for exactly what they are and whose they are. Trust that God has a *good gift* waiting for you if you'll just lean into the trial and rest at His feet in it.

Rooting Ourselves in Christ

What "gift" can you find in this storm? Where have you seen God's loving hand already at work? With whom can you share your experience of this "gift" to encourage them?

_____

_____

_____

_____

_____

Day Ten
Commit Scripture to Memory

It's officially 10 full days of Chris being unconscious in the MICU. He is off the paralytics, sedation and pain medicine so that he will, hopefully, wake up. We've seen a few signs of him doing so. He grimaces when the nurses must change tubes or move him, and the lids of his eyes change from completely shut to slightly open.

The Bible is full of scriptures meant to provide wisdom, peace, hope, encouragement, and truth to our lives. Isaiah 41:10 reminds us:

> "So, do not fear, for I am with you; do not be dismayed, for I am your God. I will strengthen you and help you; I will uphold you with my righteous right hand."

Whether you are currently weathering a storm, finding your way out of one, or just walking into one, there is one thing that will change the entire trajectory of your experience, *whatever* you're facing: memorization of scripture.

To be completely honest with you, this has never been a strength of mine. Over the course of my life, I have studied God's word, listened to Christian music and planted myself in church. However, it has not been until Chris's journey that the *importance* of doing these things has taken root in my heart. God wants me to be equipped and prepared for when I will walk through the Valley of the Shadow of Death.

During these difficult days, the verses I've read, the songs I've heard, the prayers of the greater church community and the relationship I've developed with Christ strengthen me. I fear no evil.

Do the hard work now to deepen your relationship with God so it will sustain you and give you hope, peace and joy in the difficult days ahead.

Rooting Ourselves in Christ

Find one verse that speaks to your heart, write it down below, and then choose to commit it to memory this week.

_____

_____

_____

_____

_____

_____

Day Eleven
God's Love

The medicines we gave Chris to keep him alive, combined with a month of lying immobile in a bed, has caused him to develop an inability to move his body independently. It's unbelievable to grasp the severity of his weakness. Chris continues to experience acute kidney injury and acute kidney failure.

Even though I grew up in the church, the daughter of a Southern Baptist minister, I didn't know God. I knew *of* Him but knowing *of* someone is not the same as *knowing* them, is it?

What did I think I knew of God? At that time, I knew He let bad things happen to me. He watched as I struggled and suffered. He punished me for sins I didn't even commit. I thought God was supposed to be kind and loving, safe and joyful—but my life didn't reflect any such aspects of that God.

From the time I could make my own choices, I ran far from this God who let me suffer. I ran far from the God who didn't protect me or love me. I ran far from the God who seemed to punish me repeatedly. I ran until I couldn't run anymore.

Then, slowly, God softened my heart to Him and to others in my life who had hurt me. He began to rebuild trust where it was so very broken. So, I came back—but just enough to be a "good" person, one that could "check the box" of Sunday morning attendance. I wasn't making "bad" choices, and that was enough for me. I had *huge* holes in my heart and *big, thick* walls built to protect me from being hurt again. And that worked for a while. Until it didn't.

After years of feeling lost, alone and without direction, I was ready when God left the 99 for me. I finally wanted the peace that I knew only came from Him, not from my circumstances or from the people around me. I reached a place where I wanted what only God can give more than I wanted to live my quiet, protected, meaningless life. I wanted *whatever* it *took* to become the person He created me to be *more* than I wanted the comforts of my current life. That was when I finally, genuinely, met God—not the God I had known as a kid, but the God He had *always* been, and I was just too hurt and too scared to see it.

I'm not special. God didn't meet me and begin to heal me because I'm unique or more important to Him than anyone else. He will not stop chasing *you*, calling *you*, seeking *you* and loving *you* either. All you must do is *let Him*. Let the One who made you and knows you draw near to you and heal you. You can rest and let Him do the work.

I hope my story encourages you to trust God when He calls you. To trust that no matter what life may outwardly look like, *you can trust Him*. He will carry you and sustain you. You can rest, mentally and spiritually, during the hard times while God does what *only* He can do. Oftentimes, we ask God to make life easy, but rarely is *easy* best for our character. The miracles will come, but usually He asks us to walk through the miracle with Him while we rest in the knowledge that He *is* at work on our behalf.

Rooting Ourselves in Christ

Have you mistakenly believed God is mad at you or punishing you? Have you allowed past hurts to keep you from experiencing God's love for you? How can you trust God today and walk through your miracle with Him?

_____

_____

_____

_____

_____

_____

_____

_____

_____

_____

Day Twelve
Easy Miracles

Chris was able to have his chest tube removed yesterday but continues to have one lower lung that has yet to re-inflate after his pneumothorax two weeks ago.

So often when we pray to God for miracles, what we're really saying is, "Make it easy." But what if *easy* isn't *best*? Easy doesn't build character, perseverance or strength. Easy isn't impactful, memorable and life-changing. God rarely does *easy*.

The one who *loves* easy is the Enemy. Satan wants us to live easy so we don't struggle—and therefore don't change. When things are easy, we don't have a reason or need to impact our life or anyone else's. He likes easy because easy keeps us from realizing our real need for and dependency on God. Easy keeps us focused on our own abilities and keeps us in a place where we judge others against "our" easy.

But what if God's plan to make a masterpiece of our life includes walking *through* the miracle? Walking *through* births character, strength and perseverance. When we walk *through*, lives—beyond our own—are impacted and changed. When we walk *through*, we realize what has always been true: We have a real need for and dependency on God. It is only in the walking *through* the miracle that God can finish His masterpiece in and *through* us.

Rooting Ourselves in Christ

What are you trying to avoid walking through during this storm that God may be wanting to use as the catalyst for your miracle? Instead of asking God to make it easy, pray for God to equip you for the hard work of going through this season.

_____

_____

_____

_____

_____

_____

_____

_____

_____

_____

Day Thirteen
God of the Hills and Valleys

Chris has become more aware of his condition, and the weight is clearly beginning to impact him emotionally, not just physically. He desperately wants to go home soon, which is not an option for many, many months. He struggles not being able to move any part of his body independently and being in and out of consciousness where teams of strangers talk about him but not really to him. And when they do, he retains very little of what was said.

1 Kings 20 tells the story of two kings waging war. One of the kings, Ben-Hadad, is determined to take control of the Israelites and their king, Ahab. Initially they battle in the hills, and God gives the victory to Ahab and his people. King Ben-Hadad's officials advise him that he should try to attack again, but this time on the plains or the valleys. The officials' reason that the Israelite god is a god of the hills—so if Ben-Hadad attacks the Israelites from the valley, the Israelite god will be incapable of defending them and Ben-Hadad will be victorious. God, who is not limited to hills or valleys, responds with:

> "Because the Arameans think the LORD is a god of the hills and not a god of the valleys, I will deliver this vast army into your hands, and you will know that I am the LORD."

This story reminds me of how often I put God in a box. Sometimes, God is god on Sundays but not Friday or Saturday nights. Maybe God is god in church but not at home when I'm frustrated with my kids or my husband. Maybe God is god of my quiet time but not my work time. How many years, opportunities and victories have I lost because I didn't realize God is God of *everything* and *everywhere*; not just when it's convenient for me or only when I need Him?

The idea that God is God of the hills *and* the valleys means that God is God whether He miraculously heals my husband or allows him to remain in the hospital for months battling for his life. The circumstances or events of my life don't dictate whether God is God. He either is, or He isn't. My faith doesn't change who He is, but it does change how I see things and the opportunities I give Him in which to be glorified. Only God knows the number of our days and how they will be spent. Only God knows the impact our story will have on the life of another.

If I were to write our story, would I choose for Chris to wake up tomorrow strong, completely healed and allowed to miraculously go home? Of course! In my mind, I can imagine how amazing that story would be and how awesome it would be to share it with others. But what if a story like that—one without turmoil and struggle—doesn't reach the heart of the one God is seeking? What if walking *through* the turmoil and difficulties and unknowns is exactly what allows God to reach the one whose heart has been hurt and broken? What if it's only through our faithfully walking through this storm that revival happens?

Rooting Ourselves in Christ

Will I trust God to be the god of the hills and the valleys then? Will you?

_____

_____

_____

_____

_____

_____

_____

_____

_____

_____

_____

_____

_____

_____

Day Fourteen
Out of the Boat

Chris's lungs have cultured a new bacterium, so now we wait to see what it responds to so we know how to proceed. While watching everything Chris went through this morning and watching his medical team at work around him, I was thankful, again, that I could stand at the foot of his bed and just calmly pray. I remain completely convinced that God has us in His hands and that He will bring Chris back home. When...how...what will that mean or look like, I have no idea, but God does.

I have three pivotal turning points in my walk with Christ. Three moments that completely changed my heart and my trajectory. Three moments I believe prepared me for this journey. At each turning point, God met me when I was ready to listen and when I demonstrated I wanted Him more than my "comfortable" life. The moment I was desperate for God, He drew near.

God is patient. He's gentle. He stands at the door and knocks, waiting for us to open it to Him. He doesn't knock the door down and barge in. He doesn't demand anything we're not ready or willing to give. God also won't move in our life the way we ask him to or say we want him to, until we *let* Him.

I love Matthew 14:29:

> "Come," he [Jesus] said. Then Peter got down out of the boat, walked on the water and came toward Jesus."

I love this reminder that Peter *walked on* the *water*. Over the past few years, I've grown less concerned about the storm around me, about what the people on the boat with me are or aren't doing, and about what will happen to my possessions or even to me. All I really want is for God to call me to *walk on the water with Him.*

I pray that our journey encourages you to seek God in a real and tangible way. I pray it encourages you to turn your eyes away from the storm around you, to ignore what other people on the boat are or aren't doing, and to be unconcerned about the possessions you'll be leaving behind. Instead, *trust God* and *walk* on the water *with* Him when He calls you.

Rooting Ourselves in Christ

What is holding you back from walking on the water with God during this storm?

Day Fifteen
Joy is a Choice

Chris has been able to try breathing on his own and has been more alert and responsive. The doctors were encouraged by his latest lab reports and plan to titrate down more medicines with the hopes of stopping them completely in the next few days. If his current level of progress continues, hopefully he'll be eligible to be transferred to a long-term critical care hospital later next week.

I've thought a lot about *joy* recently—probably because I wasn't feeling much of it. God is so kind in His patience with me and my lack of joy that He gave me two different people to remind me that joy is a choice, not a feeling.

It's easy and understandable to not have joy, given that we've spent nearly two months in the MICU. It's easy and understandable to find negatives or faults in my life and in others' lives. It's easy and understandable to focus on our lack of progress.

But God asks us to be different and to act differently.

God asks us to see things as He does. Colossians 3:2 reminds us that God asks us to set our eyes on things above—on heavenly things, not on earthly things. Our joy is a choice, a decision. Our joy comes from Him, not from our circumstances or our feelings.

We can find joy by focusing on the good in each day and through actively choosing to look for our "wins." No matter the circumstances, God is always there. No matter the situation, God is still sovereign. Still *good*. Still *trustworthy*.

Rooting Ourselves in Christ

If you chose joy, how would your life look different today? How could you be a light in someone else's life today amid your storm?

_____

_____

_____

_____

_____

_____

_____

Day Sixteen
Panem et Circenses

I wanted to share a small sample of some of the prayers God has answered already for our family. Chris is alive against all medical odds. He has battled back from death and from a less than 10% chance of surviving.

One thing I've realized about our journey is that God is not doing anything "special" for us that He doesn't want to do for you. But we've had all pretenses of our own abilities and strengths stripped away. The truth is, we're no more capable of fighting the battles of our *daily grind* than we are of battling these life-or-death circumstances. *No matter what's happening,* we are just as dependent on God. But when we're enduring a storm, our self-imposed blinders—the ones that lead us to believe we are in control—vanish.

God wants us to be just as dependent on Him—for His healing, His protection, His provision, His joy—on a typical Thursday morning as we are this morning in the hospital room. The location, the details, the outward appearances of our life shouldn't determine our response to God's calling, and yet it so often does.

It's easy to be deceived and not realize our genuine need for God during our *"normal"* life since we often believe we're capable of meeting our own needs. Levi Lusko refers to this as *"Panem et Circenses"* (Bread and Circuses). The basic premise is that if Satan can keep our basic needs met and keep us entertained, we won't notice he's stealing our freedom.

My prayer for you is to slow down a bit this morning and look around. Are you living a "*Panem et Circenses*" life and relying too much on the mistaken belief that you're capable of meeting your own needs? Or are you fully aware of your real need for God—even in the normal daily grind?

Rooting Ourselves in Christ

Have I allowed the Enemy to steal my freedom through believing I'm capable of meeting my own needs? Am I filling my days with "entertainment", so I don't have a hunger for God in my daily life? If so, what do I need to do differently so that I seek God and not "bread and circuses"?

_____

_____

_____

_____

_____

Day Seventeen
The Irony of Joy

We continue to experience little rest overnight, and the need for God's strength and endurance is ever present. During the last few nights, we have faced some steps backwards. Chris is unable to sleep, and he's experiencing drops in his oxygen saturation levels. Nights of little sleep lead to long, hard days when his body is too exhausted and weak to push himself physically and make the progress he needs to demonstrate to leave the MICU.

Irony is a funny thing.

For the past few years, I've chosen a "word of the year." Some years it's been a clear choice based on life circumstances—either what they were or what I wished they would be. Other times, it's been based on an inward change I wanted to make. Ironically, for this year I chose the word *joy*. Only a handful of days into the year, the irony of this word choice did not escape me.

How can I have "joy" when it looked like my husband would die— and did for six minutes? How can I have "joy" when I am not sure the extent of permanent damage to his body? How can I have "joy" when I have *no* idea how or when this will end and what our lives will look like when it does? How can I have "joy" amid children crying for a daddy that's not here? How can I have "joy" when we may lose everything? How can God *really* expect me to have "joy" *this* year while walking through *all of this*?

In Habakkuk 3:17-19 we read:

> "Though the fig tree does not bud
> and there are no grapes on the vines,
> though the olive crop fails
> and the fields produce no food,
> though there are no sheep in the pen
> and no cattle in the stalls,
> yet I will rejoice in the Lord,
> I will be joyful in God my Savior.
>
> The Sovereign Lord is my strength;
> he makes my feet like the feet of a deer,
> he enables me to tread on the heights."

Even in the middle of a complete wasteland and devastation, long *before* there is *any* resolution or tangible promise of change and new growth, God calls us to *still* be joyful. God asks His children to *trust* Him, even when our physical eyes only see loss. God asks His children to believe that even *here* and right *now*, He *is* at work, and He will *do good* on our behalf *through* all of what seems to be lost. (I think our obedience to choose joy *in* the brokenness is the catalyst that spurs God into action.)

The interesting thing to me is that God never once asks us to be "happy." There is a big difference between happiness and joy. *Happiness* is circumstance-specific. The temperature is a perfect 78°F, therefore I *feel* happy. *Joy* is different and has *absolutely nothing* to do with our present circumstances. Joy isn't feelings-based. Joy is founded in an internal trust in God. I can have joy—a hopeful, peaceful expectation in *all* circumstances—when I *trust* that God really *will do* what He says He will do, which is to work *all things* together for *my* good and *his* glory.

I can have joy in whatever I face if I actively *look* for God's hand at work *while* I'm walking *through* the hard times. If God says He will never leave me nor forsake me, then *right* now, *right* where I sit typing this, He is here. I need only look for Him. I can have joy in celebrating birthdays and anniversaries without Chris as I look up and see the love that surrounds my family during this time.

Having joy in *all* things is our choice, and it's fundamentally tied to our perspective—both on *what* and on *whom* we focus. If I walk through the remainder of this journey with Chris in the hospital focused inwardly on myself, my problems and my worries, then there will be no joy. Joy is intrinsically linked to God and to the worship of God. To experience joy whatever the circumstance, I must stay connected to the source of all joy with my heart and eyes fully locked on His.

I don't know what you're walking through, but I *do* know that *all* of us are either walking *through* a difficult circumstance right now, walking *out* of one or headed *into* one. Wherever you are, whatever you're facing, place your eyes on God—not the circumstance. As you do, He will give you strength and feet like a deer to tread over whatever mountain is in your path.

Rooting Ourselves in Christ

How can you choose joy today? How can you change your current focus, so you can experience God's peaceful expectation in this moment?

_____

_____

_____

_____

_____

_____

_____

_____

_____

_____

_____

_____

_____

Day Eighteen
From Revival to Restoration

We began our time in the MICU maxing out four blood pressure meds and having Chris's blood pressure still dangerously low, to transitioning from our last IV blood pressure med to an oral, and now to finally being able to stop all blood pressure meds. We have also gone from maxing out the space on two IV poles for more than a dozen different medicines, to one that contains just his tube feeds.

Early on in our journey, I had numerous people talk about "restoration." Friends spoke about the restoration of Chris to our family, restoration of Chris's health and the restoration of our relationship with God.

Nicki Marie Koziarz wrote in a devotional for Proverbs31 Ministries:

> "And each day God offers us a place of personal revival through the presence of the Holy Spirit. But it's up to us to step into that place, where sometimes it does, in fact, feel a little uncomfortable."

The idea of a daily restoration and personal revival is so powerful. While it's easy for me to hear the word *restoration* spoken over us and apply it to Chris and his health, maybe God is inviting me to restoration as well?

Is it possible that God is using restoration as the gateway for my own personal revival?

Throughout my life, how many walls have I put up that God wants to tear down? How much hurt and brokenness have I experienced that He wants to heal? How many times have I talked with God about a relationship that He's calling me to move from *talking* to *doing*? What if it's *my* heart, body and soul that God would like to restore, too?

Rooting Ourselves in Christ

Is God calling you to revival with Him through your own experience of restoration?

_____

_____

_____

_____

_____

_____

_____

_____

Day Nineteen
When Pre-Miracle Expectations Don't Match Post-Miracle Experiences

This journey has been mentally difficult with so many ups and downs. It's emotionally exhausting both in the room with Chris, and the times I get to be at home with the kids. It's physically exhausting going day after day with little sleep and never fully resting. It's a spiritual struggle to keep my mind focused on God and not me and my feelings.

Most of my life I've judged the Old Testament Israelites harshly. A moment here and there or a certain situation might've resonated with me, but mostly I remained befuddled at why trusting God was so difficult for them. After all, He parted the Red Sea for them, dropped manna from the heavens, brought water from a rock and dropped hundreds of thousands of quail outside their tents when they wanted meat. How do you not trust and have renewed hope in God after that?

But now, I get it. I have begun to wonder about their mindset. While they were in captivity, what, in their mind, did freedom from slavery look like? When they were walking on dry ground across the Red Sea with skyscraper-sized walls of water on either side, what did they think life would look like on the other side of this miracle? What about the first morning the manna appeared? As excited and grateful as they felt, how long did they envision having to collect it and eat it? During this 40-year desert reign, what hopes and dreams did mothers whisper into their little ones' ears?

I wonder how often our post-miracle realities match our pre-miracle expectations.

I can list a dozen-plus miracles that have brought us to the 64th day. And I can also tell you when this began in March, I expected our life to look different by now. I expected procedures to work the first time. I expected pain medicine to alleviate suffering like it did on day one. I expected that by now this miraculous journey would have us tangibly closer to our promised land.

I wonder how many times we grow weary walking through a miracle because it looks and feels different from what we expected. When the emotional high of the last "big win" wears off and we're looking at another long and difficult day, the exhaustion sets in. When our physical and emotional resources are spent and there seems to be no end in sight, it's easy to become weary. Amid our thankfulness for the manna, our hearts still long for a home-cooked, family dinner.

It's here, where real life doesn't line up with what we expected, that our faith grows. It's here, where we are spent, that God can begin to replenish us with life from an eternal source. It's here, in the middle of our own 40-year desert walk, that God is waiting for us to realize those were *our* expectations, our hopes, our dreams, our desires—not His. It's here, after we've walked through the miraculous but not yet into the Promised Land, where God is waiting to meet needs we cannot.

I can only imagine how weary the Israelites must have felt when they first glimpsed the giants in their Promised Land. That was another expectation they had to release. It's a great reminder to me now to align my expectations up with God's. When I see giants in my Promised Land, I want to see them with eyes of faith like Joshua did—so I can see what God has in store for me *beyond* the giants.

Rooting Ourselves in Christ

What pre-miracle expectations did you have that might be stealing your joy from today? How can you align your focus of how life "should" be to coincide with God's plans for you? What steps can you begin taking today so you see your giants with eyes of faith as Joshua did?

_____

_____

_____

_____

_____

_____

_____

Day Twenty
There Might Be Giants

Chris has started to fever again, and his white blood count is elevated again. This may delay our ability to leave the MICU. His kidneys are still not fully functioning so dialysis continues to be needed.

In Numbers 13, Moses sends a handful of Israelites to scope out God's chosen land and report back their findings. Verse 28 reads:

> "But the people who live there are powerful, and the cities are fortified and very large. We even saw descendants of Anak there."

It's this verse that reminds me of the *very* thing I often do. God has promised to restore us to a land flowing with milk and honey. I have proof of His power and the Promised Land in my hands. Yet all I focus on are the giants—the few obstacles that, in my mind, are too big for me to tackle. And I mistakenly place my limitations on God.

I see the giants and forget my faith should be in the One who *is bigger than any* giant. I see the walls and forget my faith is in the One who isn't bound by time and space, much less something so insignificantly small as a man-made wall. I see dreams and promises just out of my reach and forget my faith is in the One who *placed* those dreams and promises in my heart. I forget my God is a God who does what He says He will do.

How often, I wonder, am I looking for the giants and completely miss the post-miracle blessings God had planned? How often does *my* wrongful focus delay God's next miracle?

If all the men who explored Jericho had come back with Joshua's belief that God would move as He promised, would God still have delayed their entrance into the Promised Land? I'm guessing not.

How often am I standing in my own way and delaying God? I pray for God to move, and He's waiting for me to trust Him and move out of His way first.

Rooting Ourselves in Christ

Are you like the Israelite spies who saw giants? Or are you like Joshua who saw His mighty God? Are there giants you are wrongly focusing on that might be delaying your miracle? What can you do that will help you see with eyes of faith as Joshua did?

_____

_____

Day Twenty-One
Well Done, Good and Faithful Servant

We are excited to be able to finally shift our focus from life-sustaining measures to strengthening measures. We'll begin to focus more on weening him off the vent and physically rehabbing his body so we can tackle his abdominal issues next month.

Have you ever Googled yourself? If not, or if it's been a while, I highly recommend it. It's a nearly out-of-body experience to see your life (probably more than you realize) out there for anyone to read. If you Google me, on paper I look "good." You'll see articles quoting me as the President of the Junior League of Waco, references to my company Rooted Leaders, mentions of my time with other leadership development companies and nods to my work with See You at the Station. On paper, it's easy to think I'm a "good" person or doing a "good" job.

The Bible is very clear to say that one day, we *all* will have to give an account of our choices. Unlike Google, I think God's version will be less about checking our resume and more about checking our hearts. Google doesn't care how many times I was tired, frustrated, stressed, worried or upset. Google isn't tracking whether I was rude, unloving and disrespectful to my family. But God does. There's no website that lists how many times I worried more about what a stranger thought of me than what God thought of me. Google can't gauge the number of times I was willfully disobedient to God, but God can.

When I review my inward life and choices, I see a much more selfish, self-centered person than I care to admit. It's the real, sinful me that God tracks and wants to change—not the outward, worldly persona.

The next time I Google myself, I'd love to see evidence of lives I've had a hand in changing. Evidence of people I've helped along the way—people whose hearts were broken and whom I refused to walk past. I'd love to know that people's lives are better because my heart beats more closely with God's. I'd love to know that family, friends and complete strangers will be with me in heaven because of a seed I planted in their life along the way.

When I stand before God and give an account of my countless wrong choices, I hope my choosing to be obedient to God wherever/whenever/to whomever He sent me far outweighs my missteps. Since Google will never be able to tell me whether my life was truly successful in the things that matter, I hope one day I will hear, "Well done, my good and faithful servant" spoken by the *One* who *does* matter.

Rooting Ourselves in Christ

What do you want your life to reflect? Are there areas of your heart you need to more closely align with God's?

_____

_____

_____

_____

_____

_____

_____

_____

_____

_____

_____

_____

_____

_____

_____

_____

Day Twenty-Two
I Want to Be Different

The steps ahead will be slower and more arduous than before and may be more difficult to watch as Chris becomes more cognizant of the gravity of this journey. The steps ahead bring with them very real and very raw emotions from all that has been experienced and not completely dealt with regarding our time in the MICU.

This past week after school drop-off, I found myself spending the morning at a local tire store because of an illuminated low-tire-pressure sensor in Chris's truck. (I was only driving Chris's truck because the day prior I realized I needed four new tires on my car—a problem for another day.) As I was standing in line, I thought about my internal response when that light came on and about how I'm teaching my kids to react when life makes unexpected changes to our plans. Because of my instinctive response to stress and unexpected changes, I've asked God to help me be different.

I want to teach my kids to respond to life not from their natural tendencies, but instead from God's vision for their life in every situation. When you look at me, I don't want you to see me; I want you to see God's light shining through my many imperfections. I want to be a woman, a mom, a wife, a daughter, a friend that isn't stuck in my comfortable pattern or routine, but rather who is willing to walk out into the unknown wherever and to whomever God sends me. I want to be different; I want to be changed.

Rooting Ourselves in Christ

As you look at your life and the daily choices you make, are you different from the rest of the world? Is there something different in how you respond to others or the inconveniences in life that allow others to see God's light shining through you? Could God be using this season to bring your heart and actions closer in alignment with His?

_____

_____

_____

_____

_____

_____

_____

_____

_____

Day Twenty-Three
It's All About Perspective

The doctors describe Chris's physical state as basically a quadriplegic with the ability to slightly move his fingers and toes, but without the spinal cord injury. This severe weakness is a constant concern, but there's not a lot that we can address at this time other than minimal physical therapy movements.

Perspective. There are more days than I care to admit that I'm too focused on my plans and my agenda than I am about anything of God.

Earlier this week, I realized my car desperately needs four new tires. As I drove the kids to school in Chris's truck instead (mine isn't safe with those worn tires), his low tire pressure light came on. Thankfully, the leak was slow, and I was able to drop off the kids and make it to a local tire store for repairs. (As it turns out, there was a nail in one of the tires.)

Standing in line, God asked me:

- How many times do you lose all perspective over small inconveniences?
- How many times are you focused on a perceived obstacle in your agenda and potentially miss a moment with Me?
- How many times has a negative attitude kept you from receiving My blessing?

- How many times when you didn't choose to thank *Me* during your problems did you miss something bigger, I had planned?

As it turned out, God used that little nail to bless me with four new tires. While standing in line and talking to God about my negative attitude, another woman who knew of our story walked up to me and asked what I needed to have done. Without hesitation, I relayed my plight, and she immediately offered to cover the cost of four new tires!

Only God could use a nail to bless me. It makes me wonder how many times I've missed a blessing because all I saw was the nail—and didn't thank Him for it.

God's nail allowed me to get the kids to school safely— while being close enough to home to quickly repair my tire. God's nail provided for four new tires. God choosing to use a nail saved me—again.

Rooting Ourselves in Christ
Is it possible you're missing God because all you see are the nails? What are the "nails" you may be wrongly focusing on in your life? How can you thank God for them instead?

Day Twenty-Four
God Moves in the Wasteland of Our Life

During dialysis, Chris fevered off and on and experienced periods of tachycardia combined with low blood pressure. The doctor decided to place him back on full vent support. He has also cultured two new infections.

Isaiah 43:18-19 has been a foundational verse for me the last few years.

> "Forget the former things;
>   do not dwell on the past.
> See, I am doing a new thing!
>   Now it springs up; do you not perceive it?
> I am making a way in the wilderness
>   and streams in the wasteland."

There have been many seasons I find myself drifting back to "the good times." Times when on paper it looked simpler. It's easy on days like today to remember only the good of those days and forget how empty they felt.

Anytime we end one chapter of our life (by our choice or not), I think God reminds us not to dwell in the past chapter for a reason. You can't move forward or enjoy this day, and you'll miss God's hand at work in this new season, if you're looking back at yesterday.

This past week has been another difficult one. Chris has continued to have hard days with more complications while the kids and I have battled our own illnesses. It's easy to look at everything that's going "wrong" and to long for the past—to dwell on how hard and difficult today seems and to see our life like a vast desert or wasteland.

But even here in our "hot mess," God has offered new hope. It's here in the wasteland that God wants to do a new thing for me and my family—and for you. It's in our wasteland that all excess is stripped away, and barrenness exists. When our life is so full and busy, we can easily miss the small, quiet movements of God. But in the desert, you notice the small spring for the miracle that it is.

If I'm honest, I really don't want to go back to the "good ole days." I was empty there and searching for meaning—searching for God. While life is harder here in the desert, there's a miraculous beauty in the nearness of God I feel. There's a quiet optimism and hope that stems from what I've seen God already do and where I feel God leading us. In the desert, you need God to provide your daily manna. Manna that nourishes your heart and soul, not just your body.

Rooting Ourselves in Christ

What could you be missing in your wasteland?

_____

_____

_____

_____

_____

_____

_____

_____

_____

_____

_____

_____

_____

_____

_____

_____

_____

Day Twenty-Five
Rooted in Christ

Due to several new developments, we'll be moving Chris back to the MICU. His oxygen levels desaturated numerous times throughout the day yesterday and a decision was made to sedate him again in the hopes he will be able to fight off his current infections without any more loss of ground.

I am the first to admit I'm a constant work in progress. A few years ago, God pressed upon me the need to move beyond my box-checking, church-attending life and move into a *real* relationship with Him. He called me to become rooted in Him.

Recently, I spoke to a group of moms about the need to be rooted in Christ. I talked about the role of a plant's root and how that correlates to our own relationship with Christ. The depth and health of the root determines the health of the plant and the amount of fruit that plant can produce. Unhealthy roots equal unhealthy plants.

When was the last time we stopped to ask ourselves what we're rooted in? Lots of times, as "good" people, we root ourselves in "good" things. But these "good" things will not, and cannot, feed our "plant" lives. Only God's word can. Maybe we're rooted in our work trying to provide for our family? Maybe we're rooted in caring for our family, so our kids have the stable, loving home we always wanted? Maybe we're rooted in things— wanting to provide what we were always denied and felt we deserved? Maybe we're rooted in volunteering which is certainly a "good" thing?

There are so many "good" things to be rooted in, but *none* of them will provide us with *life* when we need it most. Ultimately, is our life rooted in such a way that whatever we do prospers?

- Are you rooted deeply enough in Christ that if you, your husband or your child ended up in the MICU you could trust God was in control and not worry?
- Are you rooted deeply enough in Christ that if you or your husband lost your job, you could trust God and not worry?
- Are you rooted deeply enough in Christ that spending time with Him comes before checking email, voicemails, social media or listening to the news?
- Are you rooted deeply enough in Christ that spending time with Him comes before your husband or your children?
- Are you rooted deeply enough in Christ that your faith will not wither and die, and your life would still bear fruit *in* the storm?

Rooting Ourselves in Christ

What "good" thing are you rooted in that may be keeping you from being rooted in Christ?

_____

_____

_____

_____

_____

_____

_____

_____

_____

_____

_____

_____

_____

_____

Day Twenty-Six
Standing Against the Schemes of the Devil

Ultimately, I trust that God sees the big picture; he sees what I cannot. He knows the reason behind His timing of all things. I've come to realize that God may have a very different plan I cannot see yet—one that will bring glory to Him. While I continue to pray for Chris's complete healing and for full restoration of his kidneys, please join me in praying that what we truly want is for "thy will" to be done—not ours.

This past week has felt like a battle—illnesses upon illnesses, new infections, low tires, bald tires, etc. Over the past few days, I have begun thinking about Ephesians 6:10-11:

> "Finally, be strong in the Lord and in his mighty power. Put on the full armor of God, so that you can take your stand against the devil's schemes."

What sticks out to me is the word *schemes.* If you look it up, *scheme* is defined as:

> a large-scale systematic plan or arrangement for attaining some object or putting an idea into effect.

Satan isn't randomly throwing whatever is closest to him at us. Oh no; he *studies* us. He thinks about us and creates a *large-scale attack plan* to *systematically* hurt us, so he can try and put *his specific* idea into effect.

Thinking about it this morning, I got angry. As I drove to the hospital, I no doubt looked like a crazy woman taking a stand against these schemes and telling Satan *no more*. No more will I allow him to make me feel victimized. No more will he be allowed near Chris, my kids, myself. From now on, he will encounter angels covering us and will be wasting his time. He might as well give up and go back where he came from. I will no longer listen to the lies from his slithering lips. This is *war*, and I'm ready for battle.

It's a little crazy I know, but ranting to Satan this morning—taking out my anger on him—felt powerful. I felt vindicated. I'm a daughter of the *King*, and I will no longer stand by and allow this assault to continue.

If you are facing a battle (and I firmly believe we all are), try it. Out loud—yell it if necessary—tell Satan off. Tell him how you feel and claim the authority you have over him because of Christ who lives in you. There is power in it; I promise!

Rooting Ourselves in Christ

As you review your past few weeks, what are the devil's schemes at work in your life? Which promises of God can you claim over them?

_____

_____

_____

_____

_____

_____

_____

_____

_____

_____

_____

_____

_____

_____

_____

_____

Day Twenty-Seven
Walk on the Water

We are awaiting test results from last night to see whether Chris needs surgical intervention currently to improve. Any surgery will be extremely risky and comes with a high mortality rate. We are hopeful that Chris will continue to stabilize enough so we won't have to make this difficult decision.

I've been reading the story of God calling Gideon in Judges 6. Gideon is terrified of the Midianites who have taken control of the land. In fact, Gideon is so overwhelmed with fear, he's secretly threshing his wheat in a wine-press so he can keep what little food he gathers away from the Midianites.

(I wonder how many times in my life my fear that God won't provide for me, even though He has repeatedly promised He would, has led me to ridiculous decisions like threshing wheat in a wine press? Fortunately, God is God, and hiding in a wine press does not prevent Him from keeping His eye on me—or on Gideon in this case.)

In verse 11, we read that an Angel of the Lord came to where Gideon was hiding. The Angel of the Lord says, "The Lord is with you, mighty man of courage." In just two verses, God shows us two things about His character. One, He *sees* you; you cannot hide from God. (In the reverse, you also don't need to worry about *doing* anything for God to find you. You do not live in too small of a town or have too small of a position or even possess too few abilities for God to come *to you* when He's ready.) The second thing we learn about God is that He calls things that are not (in our own human nature) as if they *already*.

As Gideon and the angel chat, the angel says:

> "Go in this your might, and you shall save Israel from the hand of Midian. Have I not sent you?"

This great declaration from the Angel of the Lord is met with Gideon telling the angel he's clearly made a mistake because Gideon couldn't possibly save Israel. To be sure the Angel understands all his shortcomings, Gideon lists them out for him: he's part of the poorest family, he's from the smallest tribe and he's the youngest.

I love Gideon. I more often feel like Gideon than not. I want to be courageous and step out on the water and lead others to Christ, but most of the time, I'm busy making sure God knows all that I'm not. I'm just from Waco. I'm just from a lower-middle class family who struggled to make ends meet. I just went to college but don't have special training or advanced degrees. I just worked as a pharmaceutical sales representative for 14 years, and I don't possess any actual marketable skills. I just tried to start a new business when my husband got sick. I just have two little kids at home and don't have tons of time. I just....

I could spend all my time telling God *all* the things I think I'm not and completely miss *two* more important lessons.

One, in my own human nature, I might be right and might be ill-equipped to do anything for God—unable to "walk" on the water. But God doesn't care about all the things I think I'm not. God isn't calling me to go out on *my* authority, but on *his*. It is not *my* ability that will change lives; it's *His*. When God looks at me, He sees past what I think *I'm not* and sees who *He is*, living *in me*. And *that's* whom He's calling.

Secondly, my current situation, my past, my amount of education (or lack thereof)—*none* of it is news to God. In fact, God specializes in using the ill-equipped and unprepared so that *all* will see it is *God*, not me, who is changing lives and walking on water.

I encourage you to see yourself as God does, as *courageous* and look for where God is calling you to get out of the boat to walk on the water with Him.

Rooting Ourselves in Christ

Who have you been telling God you're not? List who God is living in you. Remember and be encouraged by this when you think you're not enough. God chose YOU long before you chose God. He LOVES you and sees how incredibly valuable and special you are.

_____

_____

_____

_____

_____

_____

_____

_____

_____

_____

_____

_____

_____

_____

_____

Day Twenty-Eight
Knowing God Should be My Chief Priority

My poor kiddos struggled a lot last night trying to get to sleep missing. They miss their momma and were deeply saddened by my sudden absence again. Chris wasn't stable enough for me to feel comfortable going home, so I was left with my heart in pieces. My heart was broken while being pulled in so many different directions at once.

Have you ever read something that just hit you over the head so hard you needed to re-read the same passage repeatedly until it seeped into your soul? That was my experience yesterday as I was reading Priscilla Shirer's book *Discerning the Voice of God*. Here are just a few snippets from chapter 9.

> "Could it be that you're having trouble discerning God's voice because you've somehow bypassed the need to know who He really is? Have you been 'voice hunting' more than 'God hunting'? Has knowing His will taken precedence over just knowing Him? What I've often wanted to know most from God are the details—where He wants me to go, what He wants me to do, even what He wants to do for me! I've been guilty of seeking God's direction and blessing more than I seek Him. If you no longer seek Him with 'all your heart' when

things get difficult, this is an indication that you're more interested in what you expect Him to do for you than in simply knowing Him."

As I sat in Chris's hospital room yesterday reading this, I felt the sting of truth slapping me across the face. How much of my walk is rooted in my needs and not in my desire to know God? When was the last time I sought God just because I love Him and because I want to learn more about Him—not with a hidden agenda of what I want Him to do for me? When was the last time I spent time in the Word just to *understand* God better, as opposed to seeking an answer to *my* problem? When was the last time I wanted to spend time with Him, quietly and patiently waiting for Him to speak, instead of my spewing out all my needs and concerns and my list of demands? When was the last time I wasn't hurried or rushed in my time with God, when I wasn't "checking off a to-do box" but was completely present with Him? Content. Quiet. Ready to listen. Sitting at His feet just because I love Him.

When was the last time I sought God like that?

Thinking of this made me wonder when I last sought that kind of time with my husband or my kids or my friends—being fully present where my feet were. Not mentally thinking ahead to what's next or what went wrong five minutes before, but fully engaged without an agenda. Just present and content because I love them and want to know them better?

When was the last time I sought those whom I love like that?

Day Twenty-Nine
Blow Your Trumpet

The "good" news is Chris's condition is stable enough that we have time to wait before deciding on a surgical intervention option. Chris is stable enough that we don't have to choose between two losing options; we can instead wait and watch to see how his body responds. Looking at multiple factors, we have gone backwards by 2+ weeks from where we were toward the end of our last MICU stay.

I have continued to spend the last few days parked in Judges. Within a few verses of chapter six, I read about God doing what only God can do. God changes *people* and He changes *situations*.

In Judges 6:27, we read about how Gideon is fearful again—not once, but *twice*. By Chapter 7, Gideon has begun to trust God enough to fight the Midianites (the same people from whom he was hiding in a wine press a few verses prior). However, Gideon's trust in God is limited to his ability to gather *every single man he can find* to help him battle against this army. Nervously optimistic, Gideon convinces more than 32,000 men to join him in attacking the vast armies of Midian, Amalek and other nations.

But God, being God, changes the situation and tells Gideon not once, but twice, to scale down his men. By verse 7, God has decreased Gideon's numbers from

This morning I find myself, for the firs
seek God. Trusting that as I *know* Him
Him" happens. That

> "...when knowing God is [my]
> will reveal truths about Himse
> personality and His plans—tha
> toward the paths [I] should tal

Make time to seek Him. No agenda. No
Just spend time with Him for the sake
and trust that as you do, you *will* hear

Rooting Ourselves in C

How can you prepare yourself to be fully
God? How can you adjust your normal q
you're seeking God and not your agenda

_____

_____

_____

_____

_____

This morning I find myself, for the first time, ready to *seek* God. Trusting that as I *know* Him more "hearing Him" happens. That

> "...when knowing God is [my] chief priority, He will reveal truths about Himself—His personality and His plans—that will point [me] toward the paths [I] should take."

Make time to seek Him. No agenda. No specific needs. Just spend time with Him for the sake of knowing Him, and trust that as you do, you *will* hear His voice.

Rooting Ourselves in Christ

How can you prepare yourself to be fully present with God? How can you adjust your normal quiet time so you're seeking God and not your agenda?

_____

_____

_____

_____

_____

Day Twenty-Nine
Blow Your Trumpet

The "good" news is Chris's condition is stable enough that we have time to wait before deciding on a surgical intervention option. Chris is stable enough that we don't have to choose between two losing options; we can instead wait and watch to see how his body responds. Looking at multiple factors, we have gone backwards by 2+ weeks from where we were toward the end of our last MICU stay.

I have continued to spend the last few days parked in Judges. Within a few verses of chapter six, I read about God doing what only God can do. God changes *people* and He changes *situations*.

In Judges 6:27, we read about how Gideon is fearful again—not once, but *twice*. By Chapter 7, Gideon has begun to trust God enough to fight the Midianites (the same people from whom he was hiding in a wine press a few verses prior). However, Gideon's trust in God is limited to his ability to gather *every single man he can find* to help him battle against this army. Nervously optimistic, Gideon convinces more than 32,000 men to join him in attacking the vast armies of Midian, Amalek and other nations.

But God, being God, changes the situation and tells Gideon not once, but twice, to scale down his men. By verse 7, God has decreased Gideon's numbers from

32,000 to a mere 300. Only God would think 300 men adequate to fight an enemy that numbered so large they looked like "locust in the valley" and whose "camels alone could no more be counted than the sand on the seashore."

But God, being God, doesn't stop there. In Judges 7:16, we read:

> "He divided the three hundred men into three groups and gave each man a trumpet and a clay jar with a torch in it."

Did you catch that? Not only does God not need 32,000 men to take on this "vast locust army," but he also doesn't need even the 300 to do the fighting. Instead of holding a sword, shield, club or any weapon whatsoever; God instructs the men to hold a trumpet in one hand and a clay jar with a torch in the other.

God has changed the rules of the game. He doesn't need you or me or Gideon's army to *do* anything. He only asks that we obey. Whatever He instructs us to do, just be obedient in it—no matter how crazy it might sound. Gideon, the terrified man, has *changed*. The same man who felt he was the "least" of all and was "fearful" is now trusting God to secure a victory through a handful of people who are holding *no* weapons.

When I read this passage, what struck me was this: Chris and our family are in the midst of a war. We're battling diseases upon diseases and things too numerous for us to count. While both Chris and I have always tried to "fix" things, this is something we cannot fix. We do not have the tools or resources to battle our "vast, locust army"; only God does. God has taken the tools we normally would use—our weapons—out of our hands and replaced them with a trumpet and a jar with a torch inside. Basically, if God does not battle for us, we're defenseless and will lose.

What I love most about this verse are the two things God specifically put in their hands: a trumpet and a torch. Throughout the Bible, God has used the blowing of a trumpet to signal He's on the move. Walking through this journey, I'm thankful God has allowed it to be a "trumpet" of sorts to sound for others that He's still on the move. And the torch? When Gideon attacks, it's in the middle of the night. God calls each of us to be His "light" in the darkness. I cannot imagine a better visual than hearing the trumpets declaring God is on the move and then seeing His light surrounding the vast armies of darkness. I firmly believe God is using Chris and our story to be just that—a beacon of light in so much darkness.

And if you're curious what happened to the "vast armies of locust," verse 21 reads:

> "Then they just stood and watched as the whole vast enemy army began rushing around in a panic, shouting and running away."

Gideon didn't even need an army. The Midianites defeated and killed themselves. When God is fighting for us, the same is true for us-we do not need anything else but Him.

Rooting Ourselves in Christ

My challenge to you is two-fold: Consider where God is asking you to trust Him and "blow your trumpet" and be His light in the darkness. If you're unsure, ask God to show you if there's an area in your life you can use to sound to others that He's on the move.

_____

_____

_____

_____

_____

_____

_____

_____

_____

_____

Day Thirty
Being Light in Dark Places

Chris continues to have low grade fevers and issues with tachycardia. He is also routinely needing blood transfusions. Given the slow pace of any improvements, we're likely to remain in the MICU for the foreseeable future.

My kids and I were outside one morning looking up at the predawn sky and noticed one bright star shining radiantly above us. As the sky began to lighten, I kept watching that one star. The sun was almost up, and the sky was beginning to fill itself with the day's new rays when I realized something. Although I could no longer see its light, the star I had been watching was still there. It hadn't moved or changed. But as the sun's rays grew brighter in the sky, the star's brilliance and power become indistinguishable from the light now surrounding it.

In Matthew 5:14-16 when Jesus says:

> "You are the light of the world. A city set on a hill cannot be hidden. [15] Nor do men light a lamp and put it under a bowl, but on a lampstand, and it gives light to all in the house. [16] Let your light so shine before men that they may see your moral excellence and your praiseworthy, noble, and good deeds and

recognize and honor and praise and glorify your Father who is in heaven."

God is calling us to go into the darkness; not stay in the light. We do not light our lamps to illuminate a sunny day. We light them once the darkness comes. It's in the darkness that our light is needed the most. If God is calling us to be light in the dark places, how do we do that?

First, we can only *be* light when we have a relationship with *the* light. John 8:12 reads:

> "Once more Jesus addressed the crowd. He said, I am the Light of the world. He who follows Me will not be walking in the dark but will have the Light which is Life."

We must have Jesus in our life and have a relationship with Him first. If we have His light in us, only then do we have the power to shine *His* light in dark places.

Second, it means we must have the courage it takes to walk boldly into the dark places so that God's light can shine through us and give life to those who are there. It's easy to stay in the brightness of other Christians and be light to those who are like us. It's natural to be nice, kind, thoughtful, encouraging, and helpful to others who are our friends—people who would do the same for us if given the chance. But that's not what God is calling us to do. He isn't commanding us to shine our light in the light of day among other believers; rather He says we are to go out in the darkness where there is *no* light and shine *His* light there. He's calling us to walk out of our comfort zone and bring life to those still living without it.

There are an untold number of people we encounter throughout the day still living in the darkness who need our light—His light. They're desperate for someone who can bring them hope and point them back to Christ. Will we be like the lone star shining in the dark sky for them to see, or will we stay in the brightness of the sun and miss a chance to bring a new life into the Light of Christ? Whether it's our child, spouse, neighbor, colleague, or the individual sitting alone in the ICU waiting room; I want to encourage you to actively look for someone to whom you can bring light.

Rooting Ourselves in Christ

Who can you be a light to? What can you do today to help you root yourself in the source of all light?

_____

_____

_____

_____

Day Thirty-One
I "Know" Chip and Joanna

Yesterday was a pretty tough day. Chris spent several hours sicker than usual. The plan this morning is to do another CT scan to look for an explanation for an explanation why he's still so sick and continues to decline. It's indescribable what it's like to have multiple conversations with your spouse over the past 53 days who doesn't believe that he will ever leave the hospital alive.

For those of you keeping track, I'm still parked in Judges. I reread a question Gideon asked of the Angel of the Lord in Judges 6:13:

> "Pardon me, my lord," Gideon replied, "but if the Lord is with us, why has all this happened to us? Where are all his wonders that our ancestors told us about when they said, 'Did not the Lord bring us up out of Egypt?' But now the Lord has abandoned us and given us into the hand of Midian."

I understand his question. It makes complete sense to wonder why bad things happen. Sometimes, God gives us a clear answer during or after the storm. Sometimes, we won't know this side of heaven. But I think oftentimes, God uses those hard times to help us transition from *knowing* Him to *experiencing* Him.

I live in Waco, Texas. I shopped at Magnolia before it was *Magnolia*. Chip and Joanna Gaines's kids went to school with my kids before they became *Chip and Joanna*. I sat at a table in Starbucks next to Chip before he was *Chip*. I know things *about* them, but I don't *know* them. I don't have a personal relationship with them. If I passed them on the street, they wouldn't know my name, and I don't know who they *really* are.

Sometimes, we think we *know* God when we just know things *about* Him, or we know people who 'know' Him. Maybe we've been in His vicinity, but we haven't experienced a real relationship with Him. Sometimes it takes those rocky and difficult seasons for us to move from knowing about God to experiencing Him. If we never need Him to provide, heal, or answer a prayer, then how will we ever really know that He *is* who He says He is? How will we move from head knowledge to heart knowledge? How will we ever be able to trust Him and be obedient to wherever He calls us if we first haven't had the chance to experience His trustworthiness for ourselves?

As you seek God in your storm, look for a new aspect of His character He might be trying to show you. Maybe He hasn't answered your prayers yet because He's still waiting for you to experience His full nature. Maybe He wants you to know Him at a deeper and more intimate level. Could God be using this storm to help you move from head knowledge to heart knowledge—to personally experiencing who He is?

Rooting Ourselves in Christ

How could God be using this storm to show you're a new part of His character? How could God be moving you from knowing about Him to knowing Him during this storm?

_____

_____

_____

_____

_____

_____

_____

_____

_____

_____

Day Thirty-Two
A Heart Like God's

Chris is going to have another procedure later today to address some of the fluid around his pancreas as well as what is causing his vomiting. As with everything, it doesn't come without potential complications or additional tubes and drains in Chris's body. It was especially difficult to make this decision on Chris's behalf when he is understandably afraid for how it will feel and impact him physically.

In 1 Samuel 13:14, Samuel tells Saul concerning the next king:

> "...now your kingdom shall not endure. The LORD has sought out for Himself a man [David] after His own heart, and the LORD has appointed him as leader and ruler over His people, because you have not kept [obeyed] what the LORD commanded you."

If you know much about David, you know he was a man full of regrets. He had an affair with a married woman, then he had the woman's husband murdered to cover up his mistress's unplanned pregnancy. His illegitimate baby died because of his actions. On and on, David had regrets. But even knowing *all* of this, God *still* said of David, "he was a man after His [God's] own heart."

Even though my list of regrets is different from David's, I can relate to his story. Once the sun is down and the house is quiet, it's easy for me to feel never-ending regret and disappointment. Regret over what I said to the kids instead of what I *should've* said. Regret about how I spent the day trying to "get something accomplished" instead of just enjoying this moment in time with them. Regret because I didn't get done what I needed to or should have gotten done. Regret at choosing not to spend time with God.

I've come to realize that most of the regrets flooding my mind are *not* God standing over me with a disapproving look on His face. He's not shaking his head over all the ways I've let Him down—again. No, these regrets have a different source. A source that would much rather remain nameless or remain disguised as *me*. These always negative, self-defeating regrets are not God at all, but Satan.

Did I lose my temper and act out of frustration or selfish motives toward my kids? Yes. Did I focus on the wrong things in my "Martha" driven personality? Yes. Did I self-sabotage or waste time that could've/should've been spent differently? Yes. But, is God in any way mad at me or disappointed in me? *No.*

Would God prefer that He be the *first* priority in my head and heart? Yes. Would he prefer that I turn to Him before turning on Facebook or checking emails? Yes. But God doesn't want me to think of Him before all those other things because He needs His ego stroked. God doesn't want my heart to seek Him and thirst for Him more than anything else because He's a self-centered egomaniac. He wants it for *me*—for *my* benefit.

The God who created us understands that we develop *in* our priorities. How we spend time, and with whom we spend it, determines who we'll become over time. Like a marriage, we become yoked with what fills up our time and attention. Because of this, God wants us to have more of Him in our lives than any other thing. He knows that spending time with Him and learning about His nature aligns our hearts, our minds, and our attitudes with His so that we begin to reflect more of Him in our lives.

Because He loves us so much, an incomprehensible amount, that He knows the very best way for us to approach life. If I had spent time with God first, then maybe my spirit would've been softer and more at peace when my kids asked me to play with them. If I had spent time with God first, then maybe I would've been able to better prioritize my time so that the important things would get accomplished. If I had spent time with God first who knows how my day could've gone, or the example I could have modeled for my kids? You know who knows...*God*. God knows. It's *because* He knows that He wants His children to spend time with Him first so that we have the best day possible and accomplish all that He has asked of us (not necessarily all we have asked of ourselves).

Ultimately, all God is asking of any of us is to be like David and have a heart that beats in rhythm with His own. A heart that is developed over consistent and intentional time spent with Him. A heart that is soft enough to ask for forgiveness when we make mistakes. A heart that listens for God to speak and then immediately obeys—regardless of how crazy it may seem. A heart that studies God's character and trusts that He is who He says He is. Ultimately, that's where I want to end my thoughts at the end of each day— knowing I made mistakes, but also knowing my heart grew a little closer to God's and a little more of Him rubbed off on me.

Rooting Ourselves in Christ

Do you have a heart like God's? More importantly, do you have a desire to have a heart like God's? If so, what is one thing you can do differently today to help you align your heart a little closer to His?

_____

_____

_____

_____

_____

_____

Day Thirty-Three
Worn

Chris has developed a potential complication in his abdomen since having the drain and tubes placed. We're waiting on a consult to decide our next steps. His latest cultures are showing signs of another infection. Once again, we'll be adjusting his antibiotics and antifungal medicines.

Earlier today, someone asked me how I was doing. I answered, "I'm tired." What I should've said was, "I'm worn." Setback after setback, I'm simply worn.

Chris is worn. My kids are worn.

Then, I read Isaiah 43: 1b-2a:

> "When you pass through the waters,
> I will be with you;
> and when you pass through the rivers,
> they will not sweep over you.
> When you walk through the fire,
> you will not be burned"

It reminded me of a passage I read earlier this week in Daniel 3—the story of Shadrach, Meshach, and Abednego. Long story short, these three Israelite men are summoned to King Nebuchadnezzar after refusing to worship his statues. The king is so infuriated he has them thrown into a fiery furnace, the temperature of which has been increased seven-fold just because he's that angry at them. Before he does tosses them in, he asks the men if they have anything to say or if they're now willing to change and bow down to him to spare their lives. Here is their response in Daniel 3:17-18:

> "If we are thrown into the flaming furnace, our God is able to deliver us; and he will deliver us out of your hand, Your Majesty. [18] But if he doesn't, please understand, sir, that even then we will never under any circumstance serve your gods or worship the gold statue you have erected."

What I loved about this response is that they say:

1. God is *able* to rescue them.
2. God *will* rescue them.
3. But, even if He chooses not to, they will *still* serve God and not the king.

If you've read this passage, then you know a short time later the king's guards tie them up and throw them into the furnace. The fire is so hot it immediately kills the guards. But then we then learn that the king sees not three, but *four* men walking around in the furnace unscathed. Astonished, the king commands Shadrach, Meshach and Abednego to come out of the furnace at once. Daniel 3: 27b tells us what happens next:

> "The fire hadn't touched them—not a hair of their heads was singed; their coats were unscorched, and they didn't even smell of smoke!"

I feel like my family is currently walking through a fiery furnace that's been cranked up seven times hotter than normal. And yet I believe that the things entangling us—keeping us tied up and unable to go where God is calling us—are being *burned up* in this fire. We *will* walk out of this un-scorched without the smell of smoke being detected. While things look tenuous for Chris again, I believe that God *is* with us, and we *will not* get burned because He *is able* and *will* deliver us through this. While none of this makes days like today easier necessarily, God's promises do give this *worm* family encouragement that we will see *redemption win* and the *struggle end*.

Rooting Ourselves in Christ

How does the passage from Daniel 3 encourage you in your storm?

_____

_____

_____

_____

_____

Day Thirty-Four
Be Still and Rest

The active bleeding we saw yesterday in Chris's abdomen has diminished greatly overnight. We're continuing to watch before doing additional interventions. His vitals have stabilized so we're continuing our current treatment plan and will watch to see if he regains lost momentum.

Over the past few days, I've been listening to <u>Be Still</u> by Jeremy Camp. He paints this beautiful picture of someone laying their head at the feet of Jesus and resting here in this safe place. While listening to this song, I can envision myself doing just that at the feet of the One who knows my pain, my worries, my burden, and my sorrow-resting on the one who knows.

Jeremy uses a verse from Psalm 46:10 as his inspiration. When I read it, the verse struck me that this isn't a suggestion or a "nice thing to do." It's a command: Be still. And there's more to it: We're commanded to be still *and* to know that God, *alone,* is God.

> "Be still and know that I am God. I will be exalted among the nations, I will be exalted in the earth!"

Repeatedly throughout the Bible, we can find God commanding us to be still. We see it in Exodus 14:4:

"The LORD will fight for you, and you have only to be still."

Or Psalm 37:7a:

"Be still before the LORD and wait patiently for him..."

In this season of life, I need God to constantly remind me to be still because I can trust Him. I don't need to worry; He will fight for me. All I need to do is to be still and believe that He is God.

I find myself wondering how many times God looks at me with His loving eyes and says, "Beth, I'm aware of everything you need—and everything you don't yet know you need. If you will only trust Me and be patient, you will see I've got it all under control. All you need to do is rest. Just rest at My feet."

To be able to take that deep, replenishing breath fully, knowing that all is okay—that would be an indescribable relief. And that is exactly what God is telling me I can do. Breathe. Rest. Trust that He's got this. He has Chris. He's holding me. He's holding our kids in His more-than-capable hands. *Everything* that wakes me up and worries me at 3 a.m., He has *fully* under His control.

The idea of being still scares me. Often, God calls us to "take courage" or to take a step "out of the boat" and "walk on water" with Him. As a doer, I like those commands. You need something done? No problem, I'm your girl. You need me to take courage, step out of the boat and walk on water with you? Just say the word. Being still is an entirely different matter. It's difficult for me to trust that my *not* doing is the very thing I need to be doing. That trusting patiently is the "thing."

God is calling me to simply *be still and know that He is my God*. If I know that, deep down *know* that, then I'd never doubt. I'd never have second-guess being still. I wouldn't be wide awake at 3 a.m. full of worries and fears. In fact, I would look forward to those times and would trust that He is God and He will do exactly what He says He will do. I wouldn't feel worn because I could fully rest at His feet and fully trust Him to take care of all that weighs on my shoulders.

Whatever you're walking through, I hope you'll join me in learning how to be still and trust that God really does have our situation under control. All we need to do is *be still.*

Rooting Ourselves in Christ

What fears or burdens are you still carrying that you need to lay down at the feet of Jesus? What is keeping you from trusting Him?

_____

_____

Day Thirty-Five
Who Said God was Logical?

Chris continues to have increased abdominal pain and decreased spirits. The drain we put in hasn't worked, and we'll now need to take additional steps to help him improve. Unfortunately, there are very few safe options and almost all options come with potential risk and complications.

When your spouse's journey begins with stomach pain and a "straight-forward procedure" in the hospital, it's not logical to be sitting by his bedside 100 days later—with him hooked up to machines and IVs doing the work his once autonomous body can no longer do.

The idea that we so often require "logic" from God struck me earlier today. We demand to know why things happen or don't happen. We want God to move in our life in a way that makes sense to *us*. When life or God (or both) just "doesn't make sense," we feel disappointed and frustrated. Sometimes, we even struggle with our faith.

But when did God ever claim to work by our "logical" ways? When did we read examples of His "logic" at work in the lives of the people in the Bible?

Was it logical that Peter should walk on the water? Was it logical that Jesus, simply by speaking, could bring a dead girl back to life? Was it logical that Jesus fed more than 15,000 people from one little boy's lunch? Was it logical that God would have Gideon reduce an army of 32,000 to a mere 300 when they were facing an army of well over 100,000? Was it logical that God would use a shepherd boy to become king and slay Goliath with a rock? Was it logical that God would bring down a city's impenetrable walls with a group of people taking a stroll?

Was it logical that Jesus, who was without sin, loved *me thousands* of years before I was even born and chose to die one of the most inhumane deaths imaginable simply, so I can have the choice to follow Him?

Why do I think God should work using my definition of logic? Why do I so pridefully assume my definition of logic is the best? Why does my faith waiver with the decisions of a sovereign God?

Is it logical that God, who used letters from a man in jail to fill the books of the New Testament and spread the gospel, could use my random social media posts to encourage others as I share my own trials and struggles?

God does not confine and limit His power to what appears logical through my finite knowledge and self-centered perspective. God's logic is eternal and not bound by time and space. God's logic is focused on His glory—not for His benefit, but ours.

Believe me, I understand how desperately we want things to make sense. We want to have a reason why this happened or didn't happen. We want to be able to explain things to ourselves or to our kids. But in our desperation to make sense of life, it's equally important to realize how many times God moves on our behalf in completely illogical ways. We don't question His illogical ways when they benefit us or meets a need. In those times, we tout His goodness, His mercy, His love. I think it's important for us to put the *same* amount of trust in the same sovereign God when storms come, and we can't see His hand at work. In these moments, I think God is closer than we realize—asking us to simply trust Him.

In these difficult and illogical moments, God wants to remind us of all He has already done that we've forgotten about or overlooked. When we find ourselves stuck in the middle of another illogical moment and all human reasoning has failed, trust that the same loving God who illogically died for *you* long before you were even born is *just* as trustworthy and loving today. He is working and moving on our behalf—just not in the "logical" way we might assume.

Rooting Ourselves in Christ

What are some of the illogical ways God has shown you His mercy and grace? Have you allowed your need for things to be "logical" to keep you from trusting Him during the storms of life? How can remembering God's ways are not our ways bring you peace, encouragement or strength during this difficult time?

_____

_____

_____

_____

_____

_____

_____

_____

_____

_____

_____

_____

_____

Day Thirty-Six
How Serious Are You?

We had another CT yesterday: the seventh. The doctors didn't see a reason for his increased pain and discomfort the last few days. Overnight, he had a few changes in labs that we'll continue to monitor, but the consensus remains to stay the course and wait/watch and see how much the body will heal itself.

Two years ago, I felt God clearly calling me in a different direction, and today I am more convinced than ever of His hand at work in my life. Has my journey looked like I thought it would? Not at all. Have I had the outward success and tangible results I thought would have come so easily? Absolutely not. Has my faith wavered? Have I struggled? Has it been difficult on myself and my family? Definitely.

Has it been worth it? *Absolutely!* Would I trade any of it or go back to how things were before? Not a chance.

When God calls you, He is *very* clear that He wants you to "count the cost" before you decide to pick up your cross and follow Him. God doesn't want you to come because of heightened emotions; rather, He wants you to make a pivotal, eyes-wide-open decision. Twice, when I prayed about making serious changes in my life and the life of my family, I felt God respond back: "How serious are you?"

"How serious are you" is a question that requires time for thorough reflection. It requires counting the cost. If agreeing to follow Christ will lead me to difficult days financially, emotionally, mentally and physically, will it be "worth it"? If agreeing to follow Christ impacts my family, will it be "worth it"? If agreeing to follow Christ looks a lot like death and sickness and more than 100 days in a hospital room, will it be "worth it"? Am I serious when I say *whatever* the cost, I will *trust* Him to work through *whatever* my situation is for my good and for the good of my family? Am I serious when I acknowledge He will use it all to bring Him glory? Is it "worth" all of that?

My answer both times has been yes. Even now, even in our current situation, there is so much peace on the hard days because I have no doubt God is with us in this storm, and He is at work to use all of this for our good and His glory. I have no idea what the future holds, because I don't *need* to know the future. I *trust* the One who holds it.

Is following God and trusting Him easy? Simultaneously yes and no.

We often struggle to grasp and trust the simplicity of His plan for us. We struggle to trust that if God has a specific job planned for our life or a specific action He wants us to take that He *really will* make that known to us. God promises that His sheep know and hear His voice. Sometimes, we hear His voice through closed doors, a changed situation or changed feelings. Other times, it's through sound advice from a trusted friend. No matter the source, God is clear that if we do our part in consistently spending time with Him, then we can trust Him to do His part in directing our steps.

Whatever you're walking through—whatever decisions you're facing—you can trust that if you will spend time with God and read His word then He will direct your steps. Whether you "feel" it or not, you can trust me on this one. I've seen God slam doors closed that were wide open and keep doors wide open that I kept trying to close.

So, how serious are you? Have you counted the cost?

Rooting Ourselves in Christ

What comforts are you willing to give up so that you'll go wherever God calls you? Is there a piece of your life you're unwilling to give over to God? If so, what's holding you back from releasing it to Him and trusting Him with it?

_____

_____

_____

Day Thirty-Seven
Being Mary in a Martha World

Chris has been sick nonstop since his birthday in March and hospitalized every day but three. Today he had his third Endoscopic Retrograde Cholangio-Pancreatography (ERCP). We were hopeful that instead of simply swapping out the stent in the bile duct, they could also retrieve the stones. The doctor said unfortunately he still had too much edema to do more. So, we'll go back in another 10-12 weeks for his 4th ERCP.

Anyone who has spent much time around me can attest that I don't sit well. I like to *do*. There's *always* something that needs to be taken care of. Even if I'm not actively doing it, I promise you that in my mind, I'm *thinking* about all that needs to be done.

Laundry, dishes, floors, yard work, weeds—why are there are always weeds that need to be pulled and laundry to be done? My hope is you can't relate, but I'm betting you can.

Maybe it's a woman thing, or a mom thing, or a me thing, but as far back as I can remember, I've always had this never-ending to-do list. It drives Chris nuts! Given this crazy personality quirk in me, when I read the story of Jesus visiting the home of Martha and her sister Mary (Luke 10:38-42) I always find myself disagreeing with Jesus' response to Martha. (Shh! Don't tell Jesus I think He got this one wrong, but clearly, He did!)

Here's my version: Martha and Mary have invited Jesus and His friends over to their house for dinner. As any good Southern woman would do, Martha cleans her house from top to bottom, including those random closets no one ever looks in but somehow *must* be cleaned *now*. She cooks a wonderfully complicated, but "casual" meal everyone loves. It's exhausting to be this hospitable. Her home must be neat, inviting, warm and welcoming. This doesn't just *happen*. It requires work, lots of help, stress and probably some yelling at the kids: "Do *not* touch that cake; it's for our dinner guests!" Martha makes sure no one sits on the couch with the perfectly fluffed pillows, and she sends the kids to play in their rooms with a, "be quiet and do *not* make a mess" reminder. (Maybe that's just at my house.)

As Martha, whom I *totally* get, is running around trying to get everything perfect for Jesus—I mean, come on, the pressure of that—she asks Him to ask Mary to stop being lazy and help! (I've always thought that must have been an awkward conversation, but I'm assuming Martha felt like *surely* Jesus would see her side of things.) But instead of Jesus telling Martha, "I totally get it; she *is* being lazy and really should help you," He admonishes Martha for not having her priorities correct! Seriously, this has baffled me my entire life until God spoke to my heart one day.

Throughout the Bible, God tells us to sit and rest and that His burden is light. Repeatedly, He tells us to come to Him, and He will give us rest. I don't know about you, but I don't know too many women, or moms, who are overflowing in the rest department. Most of us haven't seen or experienced rest in *years*—potentially decades.

So, what is God telling us? Not to do laundry or dishes or work to feed our kids? No.

Jesus is reminding us that we have our priorities out of line. We're tired *because* we do everything else we feel obligated to do first, and then—assuming we haven't collapsed on the floor—we spend a quick three or five minutes with Him. We put the kids, our husband, the house, our friends, our careers and even the laundry ahead of God. Sure, we would never admit to that publicly, but how we live our life reflects the reality.

If that's the case, what should we be doing differently?

God wants us to live the way He created us—with our life grafted to His. He wants us to be so closely intertwined with Him that we *can* rest—mentally, emotionally, physically—whatever the circumstance. God wants our priorities to align with His and not with the Father of Lies who whispers that our value is found in what we accomplish or what others think of us.

We graft our lives with God's when we *start* by spending time with Him *first.* We allow Him to prioritize our time on our behalf, so we'll have a clearer understanding of what's eternally important and what isn't. When we spend time with God first, we invite Him into helping us better manage our day. When we spend time with God first, we allow God the opportunity to move on our behalf and potentially lift some of the burden from our shoulders. We allow room for the Holy Spirit to work. We will never know how much rest we might experience if only we started with God.

We'll never know what would have happened if Martha had sat and rested at Jesus's feet first. Maybe Jesus would have performed another miracle and the food and home would have been miraculously prepared without their assistance. Maybe the disciples would have chipped in. Maybe Mary would have told Martha to rest, and she would take care of the work.

If I'm being perfectly honest, I'll confess that I run around like a crazy woman cleaning and cooking before guests arrive because I want to impress them. I want them to think well of me. But should someone else's opinion really matter so much to me that I yell at my kids and make everyone around me miserable? Shouldn't I be more concerned about my relationship with God and with my family? Doesn't who I am and how I treat people matter more than the arbitrary cleanliness of my house or taste of a meal?

In the end, God wants us to focus on things with an eternal perspective not compounding our busyness and stress in our life doing things He never asked us to do in the first place.

As you begin to prioritize your time with God, your entire perspective will change. When I spend more and more time with God and have more of Him in me, then I begin to grasp more of who I am because of Him. The opinions of others matter less, but my desire to love them and share with them who God is in me—and who

He wants to be in them—becomes my priority, not whether a closet is neatly organized. God's strength in me allows me to rest, whatever the circumstance, in a way I could never do on my own.

Rooting Ourselves in Christ

How can you apply Jesus' desire for us to be Mary in a Martha world to your life? How would spending time with Christ first and worrying less about 'doing' feel? What's one thing you could do today to be a little more "Martha" like?

_____

_____

_____

_____

_____

_____

_____

Day Thirty-Eight
The Red Sea

Chris continues to be in a good amount of pain. The nasojejunal (NJ) tube has coiled in his abdomen so that it's not properly placed, and most everything he receives through it is being sucked back out from the nasogastric (NG) tube—including most of his medicines. Later today, we'll do another scope to help rectify this.

The Red Sea. We all have one. Maybe it's a potential divorce or a job loss. Maybe it's a diagnosis you have or one you're afraid to face. Maybe it's that "little" secret you've been carrying. It's difficult to go through adulthood without facing a "Red Sea." In Exodus 14, we learn that God delivered the Israelites out of the hands of Pharaoh only to have them facing a giant sea on one side and a furious Egyptian army on the other. All their fears were realized in this one moment as they stared at an immovable Red Sea.

For me, that Red Sea is tied to financial security. For as long as I can remember, I've had a deep-seated, lingering fear of being *destitute*. This fear has driven so many of my decisions—jobs taken, houses bought, choices made. It drove me to work three jobs while enrolled full-time at Baylor University. It's a *giant* Red Sea that haunts me, whispering its lies in the middle of the night.

But all Red Seas offer us a choice. We can either trust God to part the waters and walk through our fear, or we can become enslaved by them.

This weekend, I was reminded about the source of fear. If fear is not from God, but from Satan, then can it/should it be believed? If God is who He says He is, then shouldn't *He* be believed, despite my fear? Is it possible then that Satan, the Father of Lies and source of my fear, is using that Red Sea to entrap me and enslave me?

I have a decision to make—as we all do. Do I believe the One who has met my every need and speaks peace and joy and life into me, or the one who speaks lies and fears and death? As I stand at the shores of my Red Sea and begin to dip my toes in the water, it occurs to me that God must have a blessing waiting on the other side of this that Satan doesn't want me to have. A blessing of growing closer to Him as I grow in my faith. A blessing of real, everlasting freedom that only one who has been unknowingly enslaved in chains her entire life can experience.

Identify your Red Sea. See the fear that holds you captive for what it is and *whose* it is. Believe God's promises about your Red Sea and believe that he can and will "do immeasurably more than all we ask or imagine, according to his power that is at work within us" as you walk through it.

Rooting Ourselves in Christ

What Red Sea is holding you captive? How could God use your walking through it to draw you closer to Him and free you from what has enslaved you?

_____

_____

_____

_____

_____

_____

_____

_____

_____

_____

Day Thirty-Nine
If You Want to Know God, You Must Experience Him:

Chris continues to have issues with his NG/J tube, which is preventing him from leaving the MICU. He's also experiencing brief periods of tachycardia, low blood pressure, and desaturation overnight. Our new goal is to leave MICU (for good) next week.

I have friends who love Disney World. I mean, they *love* love it. Year after year, every chance they get, that's where they take their kids on family vacations. They can talk for hours about their favorite parts of the park and tell you all kinds of tips and tricks of what to do and not do. They have this in-depth knowledge because they've experienced Disney World several times, spending hours walking through it each time.

I, on the other hand, have only heard about it. I've seen pictures and know about it, but I've never personally experienced it. I've never set foot on the miles of pavement that make up Disney World. While I might be able to give you some information about it based on what I've heard from others over the years, I don't know about Disney World myself, and honestly, I don't think I'd trust my recall on the tips and tricks third-hand.

At some point I, too, will venture to the great homeland of Mickey Mouse, and I will envy my friends' knowledge. When I finally plan a trip for my family, I'm certain I'll find myself wishing I'd been there before.

So often in our walk with God, we want to skip over the walking *through* something and jump ahead to the knowledge and blessings we know are waiting for us on the other side. It's easy for us to read story after story in the Bible of someone having to spend countless years walking through a difficulty before receiving God's blessings. Think about it: In four short, chapters the Israelites are in bondage, then freed, then wandering through the desert, then entering the Promised Land. In one, 15-minute sitting, we skim over decades of life spent walking *through* God's plans. Whether it's the story of David, Joseph, or Abraham, it's only a few minutes before we read about God's divine hand providing the promised blessing.

In our instant-gratification world, it's easy to understand walking *through* something seems incomprehensible. We step out in faith, believing God to provide and trusting Him to part the Red Sea—only to get to the water's edge and realize just how *big* and how *wide* and how *far* we will have to cross. It seems like we're alone, so doubt sets in. Well-intentioned friends offer their words of "advice": Surely this isn't what God meant; He must have meant for you to go a different, easier route—one far more logical than to walk *through* the vastness of the Red Sea alone.

But what if He does want you to go through it? In that still, small, quiet voice that speaks deep in your heart, He asks you to do just that. God is asking you to trust H*im*, not logic or your friends or anything else, and to walk *through* the path that lays before you. It's *this* path that will develop in you the faith and obedience you need for the calling He has placed on your life. It's *this* path that He has prepared countless blessings and surprises for you that will allow you to experience, first-hand, who God really is.

What if the *only* way to *really* know God and to be prepared for where He wants to send you and how He wants to use you is to walk this journey alone with Him? Experience who He is for yourself as you walk through this illogical path.

As with all things, you can gain superficial knowledge about something through the experiences of others, but the only way you can gain personal knowledge that will strengthen and encourage you, and in turn, give you a personal testimony you can share with others, is to walk *through* this experience for yourself.

Do you really want to go your entire life reading about God? Or would you rather experience Him for yourself? The choice is yours.

Rooting Ourselves in Christ

What is God asking you to walk through? How has walking through this difficult season allowed you to experience God more fully? Could God be using this storm to teach you about His nature so that you know Him more fully? How could understanding this bring you peace and encouragement during this season?

_____

_____

_____

_____

_____

_____

_____

_____

_____

_____

_____

_____

_____

Day Forty
The Shift

Chris fevered again yesterday, so another round of cultures has been ordered. He continues to tread water— showing neither big signs of improvement nor signs of digression. His labs this morning showed a noticeable increase in lactic acid, so that's another rabbit we need to chase.

Webster defines a shift as a:

> "change in place or position or change in direction."

At one point or another, we've all had a shift. Maybe it's been a shift in an eating habit, a new show to binge watch, a career trajectory, a parenting philosophy, or a willingness to relocate to a certain city. It's hard to get too far in life without shifting in your thoughts or plans at one point or another.

Two years ago, I made a tectonic shift, or as my friend Webster would say, I "changed directions" which had "a strong and widespread impact." My shift began during a Sunday morning church service—a routine that allowed me to check a box in my Christian walk to-do list and left me wondering why I felt so lost and so empty. In fact, I had spent the past several years wondering quietly if this was really all there was for me in life. Was

I only created to be a "drug rep" who paid her bills on time? A "dependable" woman who could check all the "right" boxes and complete all the "appropriate" wifely and motherly duties? Something about this life never resonated with me.

I was nearing the end of my 40th year, the proverbial mid-life crisis no doubt looming somewhere in the corners of my brain, when I heard our pastor talk about God using ordinary people to do extraordinary things.

It was this comment that struck a deep yearning in my heart for more. I wanted *that*. I certainly fit the bill as ordinary and wanted desperately to be used to do extraordinary things. I wanted more than a box-checking life. I wanted to be someone who took risks and chased after God until He used me in *every* inconceivable way He had planned. The selfish and self-centered person I am wanted the life God had planned. Risky or not, easy or not, I wanted to be, do, see, and experience *everything* that He had in mind when He created me. I didn't want to leave *anything* undone.

It wasn't long before I realized I wanted *God*. I craved a different life. I wanted a God-centered, crazy, faith-filled, illogical life more than I wanted anything else. As this hunger in me grew, I noticed a shift. What was once important grew increasingly insignificant. What I once couldn't imagine living without became an anchor holding me to a life I didn't want anymore. This shift began small, but it grew steadily over time and continues to grow even through our current season.

I have a new-found excitement and sense of freedom as I lay down every aspect of my life and seek God's will in it. Each part of me is slowly shifting to seek His will in all I do. I'm hungry for more of God's blessings and favor. I'm more willing to release the things God never intended for me to have, and my growing trust in Him is allowing me to face a lifetime of fears that have kept me enslaved.

Do I know where God is taking me? I have no idea. But what I do know is this: Since this shift, I have more peace, more courage, more patience, and more self-control. I have more of the gifts He instilled in me decades ago but that I never fully developed.

At some point in your life, you too will have a choice to make. Will you shift toward God and the life He has planned through the narrow gate which leads to life? Or will you shift away from Him and take the easy, wider, more comfortable and popular path? Where will your shift take you?

Rooting Ourselves in Christ
How could God be using this season to shift your heart so that you depend on Him more? Where do you find yourself struggling to trust Him the most?

_____

Day Forty-One
Deep Waters

Chris was able to make great progress on the vent and tracheotomy collar for several hours. He continues to be fever-free and appears to be rid of any infection. Due to his progress and stability, Chris has been released from the care of the MICU team and transferred to a long-term acute care facility.

Since we're all friends here, can I share a secret with you? I'm not the best swimmer. My parents never taught me how to swim, and I only received a few lessons given when I was in junior high school. I swim well enough to get by, but I've never been confident enough in my abilities to feel comfortable swimming alone with my kids in deep water.

I know I'm not the only one who isn't a fan of deep waters. If I can firmly plant my feet on the ground, I'm fine. But if you get me in over my head, or when the waves get too high, fear immediately strikes. But God doesn't call us to stay in the shallow end of life. God doesn't call us to stay where we can stand on our own two feet and don't really need Him. He doesn't want us going through life where He's a "nice to have" but isn't needed. God calls us to go deep.

It's only in the deep waters when we cannot and will not survive on our own that our faith grows, and we get to meet God—possibly for the first time. It's in the deep

~ 122 ~

waters where we are utterly dependent on Him. Repeatedly, God tells us we are not in the deep waters alone. He promises to be with us. He assures us the deep waters will not overtake us. In fact, He often allows us to experience life in the deep so that we learn, personally, He really is trustworthy, and He really is who He says He is.

Ironically, after you've gone through the deep waters with God, you don't *want* to go back to life in the shallow end. You hunger for the dependency and personal connection and relationship that can be developed only in the deep waters of life.

If you're walking through the deep waters or fearful that God is calling you to go into them, trust that God loves you and wants the very best for you. He wants you to realize that everything you have, everything you are, and everything you ever will have is because of Him and from Him. While it may feel scary, unsure, or hard, He wouldn't ask you to trust Him in the deep if He wasn't able to carry you through it for your good and for His glory.

As someone who is currently in deep waters, well over my head with no end in sight, God has never failed me. God has shown me such kindness, gentleness, compassion, and a personal love like I have never known. Yes, some days are difficult, but you can trust His promise that whatever you're facing will not overtake you.

As anyone who has ever been scuba diving will tell you, there is abundant life that can only be experienced when you go deep.

Rooting Ourselves in Christ

Are you ready to go into the deep waters with God? If not, what's holding you back?

_____

_____

_____

_____

_____

_____

_____

_____

_____

Day Forty-Two
My Father Loves Me

Chris continues to make great progress on the vent weaning and has continued to show signs of his kidneys resuming function, although he's still nowhere near 100%. He has shown some increased strength in one arm/hand, but we have been told it takes about one week for every inch that was damaged neurologically to be healed. When you're 6'4" that could be well over a year.

A few weeks ago, I began writing about God's love. I wrote a paragraph or two, but I couldn't quite figure out what I wanted to say or where I wanted to go, so, I stopped. Over the past few weeks, I'd pull up those thoughts and look over them—but still stuck, I'd move on and write about something else. It's seems as though God's love should be an easy topic about which to write. While addressing our love for one another may be complicated, God's love shouldn't be. Yet, I couldn't quite get to a place where I felt I could really grasp it. God's love felt just out of reach. I could see it, but not quite grab it and examine it closely enough to fully embrace it.

If you've spent much time in church, then you've heard the phrase, "God is love." It's one of the first things you learn in Sunday School as a child. You sing songs about it and learn Bible verses that profess it. When you're young and unbroken, it's easy to accept that idea at face value. But knowing about and experiencing God's love is vastly different. And if you're an adult encountering it for the first time, it can be almost impossible to comprehend.

I don't know why I've struggled for most of my life to believe and trust in God's love. Maybe it goes back to my childhood, or maybe it's a lesson in church I skipped, but whatever the reason, really believing that God loves *me* never quite sunk in. Until now.

I've received glimpses of God's love for me here and there, but I've never felt it deep down in my soul like I have since Chris got sick. There is an indescribable experience gifted to those walking through the unimaginable. When all excess is stripped away, you experience God differently—genuinely.

We read verses about how God is our shepherd and a good father but what do those words really mean?

To me, it means that God loves *everything* about me. He delights in me. Even writing that is a new personal revelation. I look at myself and the choices I make and question God's sanity to take delight in me; and yet, He does. And God's love isn't just tied to the big things in my life. He knows what makes my heart smile, so all those things—even the tiny, insignificant details, matter to Him.

God, my Father, cares so deeply for me that while Chris can't send me flowers—one of my very favorite things to receive—God ensured I had flowers on both

Mother's Day and our wedding anniversary this year. God, my Father, cares so deeply about the silly things that make my heart happy, like a clean and organized house and beautiful flower beds—things that have absolutely no tangible value to anyone or anything except my happiness—and He speaks to the heart of individuals around me to gift me these things. Only love would care this much.

If God is love, and if God cares this much about insignificant things that make me happy, then why should I doubt or question His ability to provide for my family during this difficult time? If nothing escapes His attention, then why would "more important" things like house payments, utility bills, gas, and groceries slip through His hands? Why would a loving Father not provide for His child during this time?

If God is love, and if He has placed a yearning in my heart to speak about God to others and to lead them back to Himself, then why would I worry about His ability to open a door for me to do so?

I think I have wasted far too many years undervaluing God's love, attention, and affection for me. I have mistakenly linked God's love to circumstances or to my performance, and I've never fully grasped that His love is not tied to either. Why? Because God's love has absolutely nothing to do with me; rather, it's *who He is*. God cannot help but love and be love. He cannot help but bless, care for, and provide for His children. While we live in a fallen world and God does allow difficulties in our lives to bring us closer to Him, He is love—regardless of our feelings.

Seeing God go to such lengths to personally love me and my unique heart through these "insignificant" gifts has helped to heal so much brokenness within me. Only God would know just how meaningful the time and effort and energy of these precious friends who have given these things to me would be.

If you're struggling to believe that God loves you or that He cares about your situation, keep leaning into Him. Look for the small, tangible signs of His personal touch on the things that matter the most to you. There is nothing about you that escapes His notice. There is nothing about you that He does not take delight in. He sees *you*. And because He is love, He cares for every aspect of your heart and your life.

Rooting Ourselves in Christ

List all the ways God has shown you He loves you during this storm?

_____

_____

_____

_____

Day Forty-Three
Unlabeled

Chris has developed another fever, which means another round of cultures. We're continuing to battle tachycardia and blood pressure issues which also are impacting his ability to wean off the vent. In less than two weeks, Chris's Acute Kidney Injury diagnosis will change to Chronic Kidney Failure—with less than a 30% chance his kidneys will ever recover.

It's tough to enjoy this time of year without Chris. Small things that once escaped my notice are now pointing to his absence. For example, when Chris cooked for our family, the meal centered around something he'd grill. Somehow, I can't bring myself to use that grill without him. Chris loved to take the kids swimming. The idea of taking them swimming without him is just another Everest-sized reminder of his absence from our lives.

I'm not entirely sure how to find "normal" for our family when I can't even put a label on our situation. I'm not a single parent; yet I am. I'm not divorced or a widow; yet I have no "husband." My children have a father; yet, they don't. Shows that portray a parent who has died seem to hit a little too close to home for all of us; yet, we haven't experienced that permanent loss. There is no time off for me when I'm tired, stressed, and having a tough day. If the kids are melting down, there is no one else to lean on or to take over; yet, there should be—used to be—but now, there isn't.

We have schedules and routines, but they all center around trips to the hospital. I have an overwhelming need to take a vacation—even just a day trip—but there's no possibility of that happening. And I can't imagine going on vacation without Chris.

Regardless of how we spend our day, we're swallowed up in a deep hole. There is no "moving on" for us; we're perpetually trapped in this moment. There is never a moment when we can forget who is absent from our daily life and missing from the sidelines.

Chris's truck is still parked in his spot in the driveway. His clothes still hang in the closet. His cologne still sets unused on the bathroom counter. Yet there is no need for any of these things, and there won't be for the foreseeable future. After months of idleness and a possibility of countless more, how long do I wait before I discard or make changes to things that still belong to him? Time is marked by long days that have turned into long weeks that have turned into long months that are turning into long seasons of the year. We once watched lab results daily; now we're looking for trends over the months. He's making so little improvement. More dominoes are falling as his acute condition turns chronic. It's hard to hold onto the same hope we once had of his coming home this summer; at this point we're not sure if he'll come home this calendar year.

There are no books or resources to help you prepare to live life in this limbo. There are no checklists to help you know how to move forward when life is indefinitely stuck. There are no experts to help you navigate what to say when your kids talk about their father in the past tense or forget to mention him in their prayers because he's been absent for so long.

But what I do have in these unlabeled days is a Father who *does* know. A Father who *does* see. A Father who is walking *with* us in this and through this. I have the faith and hope that our loving Father can guide our missteps and keep us on *His* path. I trust He will continue to fill in all the overwhelming gaps of loss we experience along the way. I believe He will grant me His wisdom and grace and patience when I'm beyond exhausted and have no idea where to turn. I trust that His word is true and that He *really is* fighting for all of us. I have faith that all He is asking me to do is be still and rest and believe that He is doing everything I can't.

On these unlabeled days, I cling not to what I can't name but to what I can. To *whose* I am and who I am in Him. On these unlabeled days, His labels for me— daughter, righteous, chosen one, called, beloved—are enough.

Rooting Ourselves in Christ

Amid your storm, what labels are you struggling with? Who does God say you are? How can His labels bring you peace and comfort in this difficult time?

_____

_____

_____

_____

_____

_____

_____

_____

_____

_____

_____

_____

Day Forty-Four
Beware of the Weeds

Our time post—MICU may be short-lived. Chris has once again, developed another infection—this time a "super bug" called vancomycin-resistant enterococci (VRE). So, we've taken a few preventative steps and are monitoring him very closely for any indication we need to go back, again, to MICU.

There's something powerful about sitting outside and breathing in God's beautiful handiwork. I feel a calmness and peacefulness as I admire flowerbeds expertly planted and pruned. Serious gardeners spend countless hours carefully pulling weeds from the soil, and they know exactly which plant to place where for optimal growth. I could spend hours just admiring the beauty of someone else's work while wishing mine looked the same.

Instead of walking through lush grounds with magnificent gardens, I walk across my partially watered yard and see tangible signs of neglect. I sit on my porch and list all the very good reasons why I haven't given my flowerbeds the attention they deserve. All the excuses I list won't change the reality that I'll never see the results I long for if I don't put in the necessary time to produce continual results. Weeds, partially watered grass, and overgrown plants remind me what happens when my priorities change.

If you've spent much time gardening, you know weeds are opportunistic and can sprout up seemingly overnight. They don't grow slowly over months, but in what feels like just a few minutes of inattention or distraction. The beauty I crave will only come from a daily and consistent focus.

Our faith is no different than the flowerbeds I admire. Going to church or sitting in a small group Bible study is a wonderful way to be exposed to the beauty of God, but without putting in the effort for ourselves, we'll never see the tangible results of His work in our life.

In the quiet, vulnerable moments before I drift to sleep, I often come face to face with the weeds that have grown in areas of my neglect. In these moments, the Enemy's whispers are the loudest. My mind, if I let it, shifts to the legitimate worries and concerns I have. If I'm not careful, I start to list every bad thing that can logically happen to my family in the months ahead. It's during these dark hours that the Enemy strategically whispers his lies when I've been too busy to consistently spend time with God—and now weeds have grown from my neglect and distraction.

I've learned some key lessons regarding the Enemy's whispers. First, if I *allow* the thoughts to linger, then I become too anxious and fearful to rest. And yes, I said, *allow*. The Enemy can't make me think anything I don't allow. He can whisper all he wants, but it's my choice whether I listen and let the thoughts in, or if I immediately dismiss them for the lies they are. In the beginning, it may seem impossible to control, but as you practice not allowing every thought that enters your mind to stay, but rather "take captive every thought to make it obedient to Christ," then you will see the whispers for the deceptions they are.

Second: Taking your thoughts captive is a great first step, but to make them obedient to Christ requires that you *already know* what God says. In both Matthew 4 and Luke 4 you can read Satan tempting Jesus. With every temptation, Jesus responds with, "It is written," He's quoting to Satan what God had already spoken in His word. From personal experience, this is a hard thing to do if you haven't memorized verses and hidden them in your heart. It's hard to tell Satan what God says if you only kind of, sort of know what God says. It's hard to make Satan's lies obedient to Christ if you haven't made yourself obedient first.

There have been many nights when those whispers of fear have come, and I've let my guard down, leaving me to struggle with finding peace or rest. There have been many nights when those whispers come, and although I know they are lies, I can't quite remember God's promises well enough to squelch the fears. It's during these moments that I've realized just how important memorizing God's Word is. It's not a nice thing to do; it's a requirement if I intend to continue to battle Satan and his army of lies successfully.

So much of the stress, struggle, and turmoil we face are weeds we've allowed to grow during our neglect of a daily quiet time with God. Each of these grows from the deceits we allow to take root in our thoughts. Whatever situation we're battling, there is a scripture that will give us the answers and support we need for our victory against the Enemy. It is up to us to make knowing God's word a daily priority so we, too, can expertly pull each of the Enemy's lies up by the roots, make them obedient to Christ, and then sit in peaceful serenity as we survey the beauty that God has masterfully created in and through our spiritual garden.

Rooting Ourselves in Christ

What lies has the Enemy whispered to you during this storm? What are some of the promises of God you can memorize to combat these lies?

_____

_____

_____

_____

_____

Day Forty-Five
Looking Beyond

Chris's hemoglobin levels have dropped again requiring another blood transfusion, and he continues to battle the buildup of bile which leads to profuse vomiting. This infection has weakened him such that he's unable to progress on vent weaning and has remained very lethargic and asleep, almost continuously, since Friday.

Quitting is easy. It's easy to look at my life and think it's always going to be this way and want to quit. It's easy to look at my worries and fears and think it'll never get better. It's easy to focus on all the things going wrong and all the ways life is hard. Giving up is easy.

What's difficult is looking beyond. When my days are spent sitting next to a hospital bed, it's difficult to look beyond this season to a brighter future that lays ahead. When I'm not sure how to pay the bills and what that will mean for my family, it's tough to look beyond the worry and fears to the God who has a history of providing miracles and performing the impossible.

But that's who God has called us to be—people of vision who see beyond our current circumstances. People who see beyond the encompassing Egyptian army and the Red Sea to freedom. People who see beyond the walls and giants of Jericho to the Promised Land. People who see beyond the vastness of the Midianite army to the victory God has given through our shining lanterns and trumpets. People who see beyond the chains of the prison cell and share Jesus with a world through our New Testament writings. People who see beyond hope dying on a cross to eternal life found in His Resurrection.

God is seeking people willing to see beyond. People willing to walk forward in faith and trust that He really is who He says He is.

God has handed each of us His book with countless stories that teach us and remind us about His nature and His character. Our God isn't a God of just the Bible. He's a God of the here and now. He's both the God who parted the Red Sea and provided, daily, for hundreds of thousands of people *and* who works on our behalf today. God doesn't change. The God who fought on behalf of Joshua, Gideon, Moses, Elijah; the God who provided for the Israelites, the God who healed the blind and brought the dead to life is the same God we serve today.

All God asks is that we open our eyes to Him, so we can see beyond today's battle to the victory He already has for us beyond this moment. He wants us to keep walking with our eyes focused on Him, trusting that the same God who was with His people in the Old and New Testament is the same God who is with us today.

Rooting Ourselves in Christ

What is keeping you from seeing beyond your circumstances and trusting God? Where are you focusing that could be preventing you from seeing Him move?

_____

_____

_____

_____

_____

_____

_____

_____

_____

_____

_____

_____

_____

Day Forty-Six
Live Expectantly

Chris continues to remain lethargic even though he is not on any sedatives. He continues to have bouts of vomiting, and we're not sure why since all feeding has been suspended for a few days now. His lungs, which were once clear, are beginning to show signs of inflammation again. We're hopeful the CT can help guide next steps and help us properly treat his VRE.

Three pregnancies and two kids later, I would never claim to be an expert on having kids. In fact, I often jokingly suggest people use my life as the cautionary tale of what *not* to do. But I think there are some general principles for most pregnancies we can all agree upon. Once you've been told you're pregnant, you make different choices; your goal becomes to do everything you can to be as prepared as you can be for the arrival of what you've been promised is coming. Once you've been told you're pregnant, you wait "patiently," but expectantly, looking for signs of the arrival of your baby. Once you've been told you're pregnant, even before anyone else can physically see evidence of the new life growing inside you, you don't doubt or question the authority of the one who told you; instead, you simply *believe* them until you can hold the proof of the promise in your own hands.

I wonder how many times God has promised a miracle in my life, and I treated His promise with less authority than the man who delivered my babies? How many times has God whispered to me that He's at work—He's in control; He's working everything out for my good and His glory—and when I didn't see immediate proof, I doubted and didn't believe? I wonder how many times God has said, "Just trust me, as much as you trusted your doctor, to deliver my promise to you." How many times has the proof of God's miracle not arrived because He's waiting for me to prepare to receive that miracle—like I prepared for the birth of my children? How many times has my failure to take those expectant steps to *receive* His promise delayed the *arrival* of it? How many times have my doubts and actions told God I won't? I can't. I don't believe You until I see it for myself?

We're 130+ days into Chris's journey, and I find myself wondering what I've missed. How often God is waiting and ready to answer my prayers, but I stop looking for His answer as soon as the words have left my mouth? How often have I asked people to pray on our behalf, and then I've failed to fall on my knees and prepare to receive His answer? How often have I missed receiving God's answer simply because I haven't been actively expecting one?

I've reached the conclusion that the worst thing that can happen if I expectantly wait for God's promise is that I walk in hope. I walk in faith. I walk in peace. I walk forward throughout my day seeing all the ways God is already moving in my life that I've previously overlooked.

Whatever you're walking through, whatever you're asking God for, *expect* to see Him answer. Expect to see God's hand *already* at work in your life while you're waiting on His promise. Whatever you're asking God for, *live expectantly.*

Rooting Ourselves in Christ

What promises are you trusting God for? How can you practically live expectantly? What would that look like in your life?

_____

_____

_____

_____

_____

_____

_____

_____

Day Forty-Seven
When Praying Doesn't Work

It's been almost a week since Chris has had any nourishment through the tube feeds. We're hopeful to be able to successfully resume those later today after dialysis. For now, he's holding steady.

What do you do when prayer doesn't work? Rather, what do you do when it feels and looks like prayer isn't working?

I didn't sleep well most of last week; I was too anxious for Thursday to arrive. Chris and I spent time earlier in the week discussing how we both sensed a change was coming. We both felt something new was nearing— perhaps we were ending this chapter of illness and infections and getting ready to begin a chapter of healing and recovery.

And then Thursday came.

We received message after message from friends praying for us, for Chris, and for the doctors. Chris and I prayed together, believing the doctors would finally be able to retrieve the stones lodged in his abdomen— the root cause for most of his battles. Then the news came that there was just, *still,* too much swelling. Our only option was to replace the stent in his common bile duct and try again this fall.

Sucker punched. Disappointed. Shocked. Bewildered. Sad. And questioning God. Why wasn't He healing Chris? Why wasn't He at least allowing this *one, small step* toward recovery? Have all our prayers simply been ignored? How am I supposed to respond when it looks like our prayers haven't worked, that God hasn't been listening, that He's not moving on our behalf?

Amid my disappointment and sadness, I realized we had a choice to make. We could choose to trust God—even in this. We could choose to trust that God is still God, and He knows what we don't. We could choose to trust that even though it *seems* like God's isn't healing Chris, that doesn't mean He *isn't*, and it doesn't mean God is any less good.

Our faith becomes real in our disappointment. It's easy to trust that God loves us and is a good God who is fighting for us when all signs agree. But, what about when they don't? Is God any less in control or any less loving or any less good then? Either God is God, or He's not. Our circumstances, and our feelings about our circumstances, do not change *who He is.*

John 11 tells the story of Jesus's close friend, Lazarus, who has become gravely ill. Upon hearing his friend is dying, Jesus waits two days before making the two- or three-day journey back to Lazarus's home in Bethany. When he arrives, Lazarus has already died and has been entombed.

It's easy to assume Jesus didn't care that much for Lazarus since he waited two "unnecessary" days before going to him. But if you read earlier in John, you learn how deeply Jesus cared for this man and for his sisters, Mary and Martha. Jesus didn't want any of them to be heartbroken over the death of their brother and his friend, yet He allowed Lazarus to die. Then we read John 11: 35-36:

> "Jesus wept. Then the Jews said, 'See how he loved him!'"

Jesus wept over his dear friend's suffering and then over his loss. He shared Lazarus's sisters' pain. Both Mary and Martha knew Jesus could have saved him had He been there, and they told Jesus that. But he *wasn't* there, and He allowed this close friend to die. It wasn't because Jesus was *uncaring,* though. Even knowing what was coming He was still so broken that He, Himself, wept.

There are times when all hope seems lost and it seems prayers have gone unanswered, and it looks like miracles have died. And in those times, we weep. But you see Jesus allowed Lazarus to die because He needed the people to see how God's glory isn't limited to the physical world; it reaches even beyond death. Jesus needed us to see that *nothing* can separate us from God—not even death. Jesus allowed Lazarus to die so He could call His friend back to life long after all hope had been lost.

I don't know why God didn't allow Chris's body to show signs of healing, so his stones could be removed. But I do know that in *all* things we have a choice. I know that it is only when it seems that prayers aren't working that our faith is truly realized. We can choose to walk in our disappointment and discouragement and sadness, and we can doubt God is in control. It would be easy and even understandable to do so. Or, we can make the harder choice and trust that we *still* serve a loving God even in this disappointment. We can trust that God weeps *with* us and believe that He *will* use even this for our good and His glory—revealing even more of Himself to us and through us. We can *choose* to believe that if God wills, *nothing* is beyond His reach—not even when all hope has been lost.

As you walk through your disappointments, *choose* to keep trusting, keep believing, keep praying. Choose to believe that God is at work even when we don't see it—*especially* when we don't see it. Regardless of how things may appear, hope is not lost.

> "May the God of hope fill you with all joy and peace in believing, so that by the power of the Holy Spirit you may abound in hope".
>
> -Romans 15:13

Rooting Ourselves in Christ
Write down what you are trusting God for. Write down any areas where you have doubt. Don't be afraid to give your doubt to God. Which verses can you claim to keep

you encouraged while you wait for God to move in the places of your faith and the places of your doubt?

_____

_____

_____

_____

_____

_____

_____

_____

_____

_____

_____

_____

_____

Day Forty-Eight
Kingdom Work

Chris had a pretty difficult afternoon with significant amounts of nausea and vomiting. We had to reinsert an NG tube, suspend the feeding again, and switch to total parenteral nutrition (PTN). Because of the vomiting and the excess fluid, he has gone back on full vent support and has been unable to "speak" in over a week.

It doesn't take very much time hanging out with me before you can make a list of my many flaws. My kids will tell you to place a GoPro in our car, and you'll see those flaws for yourself in all their grandeur. While the list is long, my lack of patience is likely towards the top. (Hence the need for a GoPro so you can watch as I try, unsuccessfully, to model patience for my kids about everything and everyone that makes me nuts when I'm driving.) Let me just offer a blanket apology on that one now and promise you I really am trying to get better.

My lack of patience, my insecurities, my lack of abilities, my *very long* list of *lack* isn't new information to God. While I'm not entirely sure what He was thinking when He stitched me together, knowing all I would lack— He chose me anyway. (Clearly, He likes a challenge.)

This Sunday, our pastor encouraged us to look at what we're doing with our lives and assess whether it's "kingdom" work. Is the room you walk into different because of the presence of God that goes with you? Can anyone else tell you are a follower of Christ based on how you respond to them? (Clearly, I have a way to go with this one.) Or are we so focused on making sure our salvation box is checked that we're not actually *doing* anything with our salvation or with our lives?

When Jesus told his disciples in Matthew 9:37, "The harvest is plentiful, but the workers are few," Jesus was talking about me. I wasn't "working" on His behalf. Two years ago, I realized part of wanting more in my life was wanting God to use me for more. I realized that I wanted to go and do wherever and whatever He asked of me. I wanted to be a part of *His* harvest. I wanted to live a life that was purposeful *more* than I wanted ease or comfort. (Sometimes those prayers come back to haunt you.)

While I'm not entirely sure how Chris's situation will benefit His harvest, I do think He's using it. I can't fathom to guess what God will have us do once Chris is home or where He will call us, but I do know He's not done writing our story. Even during all these hard days, my greatest desire is to know that God is using me to encourage His laborers to go out into the harvest. I cannot wait to go wherever He can use me and all my lack.

I think there comes a time in each Christian's life when we must make a choice. Will we be willing to be used by God, however/whatever He asks of us? Or not? If Chris's and my journey can play a role in God's harvest by encouraging other workers to step out where God is calling them, then I'm so thankful He has allowed us the privilege of this journey. If our staying in this season is planting seeds in the lives of others for God to use, I'm thankful that our God, who didn't need to use such an impatient girl, chose to anyway.

While God continues to work in me, I'm looking forward to seeing His harvest produce "immeasurably more than all we ask or imagine, according to his power that is at work within us." Won't you join me?

Rooting Ourselves in Christ

What kingdom work is God calling you to do?

_____

_____

_____

_____

_____

_____

Day Forty-Nine
Resting While We Work

We continue to just run in place without being able to make much progress on Chris's ability to breathe independently or improve his kidney function. Emotionally, he's been down. This is taking a pretty substantial toll on him emotionally.

When I fill so much of my time driving up and down the same stretch of road, I tend to think and pray about all we're walking through. It was on one of these trips when I began wondering how exactly I am supposed to "be still and let God fight for me" when our family has so much need. Does that scripture mean to pray and do nothing else to solve my problems? Does it mean to do my part to actively fix my problems *while* I pray? Does it mean some other combination? How exactly do I remain "still" when I'm drowning? How can I avoid fighting with all I have left and just "trust" that it will all work out?

The Bible, at times, seems full of contradictions. In one verse we're told to be still, and in another, we're told to work. For example, Proverbs 12:11 states, "Those who work their land will have abundant food, but those who chase fantasies have no sense." So, which is it? Am I supposed to work and not be still? How am I supposed to rest in God while still "working my land" so my family will have "abundant food"? While I am still wrestling with this one and may very well not have a clear answer until we're long past this season, I realized a potential answer on my daily commute to the hospital.

It occurred to me as I was driving that the very act of driving might be the key. I actively make choices of where I'm driving, how I'm driving, if I'll text and drive, or if I'll wear a seatbelt. To drive back and forth requires a good bit of "work" on my part to successfully arrive at my destination. I use all my experience and knowledge of safe driving practices when I'm behind the wheel. Simultaneously, I'm resting. I rest in the assurance that my car won't run out of gas and my tires won't deflate and a car won't swerve into me. I rest in the assurance that the car will go where I steer it and the brakes will work when I press them. I rest in the knowledge that if I do my part in making good choices, God will do what I cannot and ensure my safe and successful arrival. I work and rest simultaneously. Along the drive, there are an untold number of ways God may be fighting on my behalf—perhaps nudging the driver I'm about to pass so they look up from their phone just in time to prevent them from swerving into me.

Is it possible to take these same lessons and apply them to my daily "work" life? Can I do my best to take my knowledge and experiences of things already in my hand and steer each in the potential best direction for my family *while I rest* in the knowledge that *only* God can open doors for my family and me? Can I rest in the realization that only God can prompt people to respond? Only God can soften hearts and give me favor so I can successfully provide "abundant food" for my family. If I work hard to do what I know to do, then I can rest in the assurance and promises of God that He will produce a harvest for us.

Rooting Ourselves in Christ

If you're struggling with the idea of how to "rest" and "work" as you trust God to move, how can you work out this Biblical "contradiction" too?

_____

_____

_____

_____

_____

_____

_____

_____

_____

Day Fifty
The Wall

Chris is not resting well at night and that has negatively impacted his ability to breathe independently from the vent. Not sleeping well at night leads to him being physically and emotionally exhausted during the day so not much progress is made.

When you simply cannot go on unless something changes, you've hit the wall. At the wall, you come to the end of yourself and your resources. Most of us who've been there didn't relish the experience and don't actively seek to go back. But when there is no more of you left to spend, to give, to share, to have, *that* is when you can experience God like never before. I truly wish it didn't take "hitting the wall" or "hitting rock bottom," but for many of us (like me), it often does.

I've spent the last several days allowing my emotions to keep me captive here at the wall. Feelings of despair, disappointment, frustration, worry, anxiety, stress, exhaustion, and loneliness have ruled my choices and my thoughts. It's easy to give yourself over to the emotions and before you realize it, they're pulling you under. Maybe exhaustion creeps in first and makes it a little easier for disappointment to welcome the lies of anxiety and stress. Whatever the situation that caused you to hit the wall, I want to share something I've learned from my time here.

Your focus matters. What you give attention to magnifies, so what you focus on matters—maybe here at the wall more than at any other time.

When you're in a low place and focused on all the things going wrong, on all the hurt, or on all the tears you've shed, it's important to remember that what you're focused on isn't the only thing there with you. There's more. There's *always* more. While the hurt and the frustration and disappointments and exhaustion are all real, there's still more.

There's God.

This isn't some platitude response meant to minimize our difficulties; it's a fact. Sometimes, when you're staring straight ahead at that impenetrable wall stretching miles to the left and right, all you see is wall. But eventually, if you step back just a bit and look up, you see that even this impenetrable wall ends where heaven descends. It's only after you've emptied your own abilities trying to do it all, and you've hit the wall that you'll finally have room for God to do what only God can do.

At the wall, He can bless you so specifically and personally that you feel immediately humbled by the extravagance. Here, God can lift your eyes to see *every* time you blew past His miracles and His provision for you in your hurry to "fix" things on your own. At the wall, when you have *finally* stopped moving, He can hold you in such a tangible way that all your hurts and sorrows are forgotten. Here, the scales that have been building over your eyes for days or weeks or months or years can finally fall away for you to see *clearly* your life, His goodness, and your blessings.

There's beauty and peace to be found here.

There's something else found at the wall: a choice. It's up to you to decide if you'll share with others the story of your time here. If you allow Him to, God can use *your* time, *your* experience, *your* revelations found at the wall to help countless others in their own journey. You can choose to praise God here and use your "wall" to break the chains of others.

Acts 16:25-26 tells us about Paul and Silas's choice at their "wall":

> "About midnight, Paul and Silas were praying and singing hymns to God, and the other prisoners were listening to them. 26 Suddenly there was such a violent earthquake that the foundations of the prison were shaken. At once all the prison doors flew open, and everyone's chains came loose."

It was the *prayers* and *praise* from Paul and Silas while shackled in prison that broke not just their own chains, but the chains of *everyone who heard them*. How you respond at the wall, and the choices you make there, will give you the opportunity to be a chain breaker for someone else, too.

While I wouldn't want anyone to walk this road, we're on, I realize it's *because* we're on this road that I've grown and changed. It's because of this journey that I trust and see God as He has *always* been; I just never realized my need for Him, so I could experience Him. Sadly, sometimes we can't experience for ourselves, first-hand, until we walk through a fire that burns all our excess away. It's because of what we've walked through that the Bible has become real to me; I now understand why Paul feels so compelled to praise God—even in a prison cell.

If there is any way for the Bible and God to become as real and as personal to you as He has for me, other than to walk through a fire, I encourage you to seek that out. But if it requires you to walk through what feels impossible, do it gladly and with your eyes on God. I promise you, He will meet you in a way you have never experienced before. It really will be a gift to be able to come to the wall.

Rooting Ourselves in Christ

What is your "wall" experience?

_____

_____

Day Fifty-One
Delayed Obedience

Chris was more awake and coherent this morning than he has been in several days. We still aren't seeing any signs of resumed kidney function, and we're very close to reaching the 90 days of acute kidney failure's progression to a permanent diagnosis of end stage renal disease.

My kids can tell you that I often use the phrase, "delayed obedience is disobedience" when I ask them to do something, and they don't immediately obey. As a parent, I *expect* my children to obey. I prefer when they choose to do so with a good attitude, but since they're 4 and 9 years old, that might be pushing my luck some days.

When they choose to obey immediately, it shows me several things about their character and about our relationship. When they stop the show or set aside the toy to get up and respond to my request, it tells me that not only am I important to them, but also our *relationship* is important. Their response shows me they honor and respect me and the authority I have over them. Their response shows me they seek to please me and want to do their part to ensure nothing comes between us. Their response shows maturity and a willingness to be appropriately submissive to me. Their response tells me they have heard my request and are willing to sacrifice their current moment of pleasure to obey without hesitation. Their response tells me they trust me and my judgment enough to immediately fulfill what I am asking them to do—regardless of their own opinions of the importance of the task.

Ironically, it's this same lesson God used today to remind me of my disobedience to Him. He has been working on my heart about an area I needed to address (a topic for another day) and yesterday, I felt compelled to act on it. But I delayed, reasoning that if it was on my heart *today*, I'd do it. Even after God had brought the idea of delayed obedience really being disobedience, I *still* didn't immediately obey. I continued to reason with myself that it was really a small thing and no one else even knew about it so what would it matter if I waited just one day? I convinced myself that because it wouldn't make a difference to anyone *that day*, but it could potentially put me in an awkward spot, I should sleep on it just to make *sure* God *really* meant for me to do this. So, I disobeyed and delayed until today to gauge the level of importance at that point. To be completely transparent, even when I remembered this morning, I *still* didn't respond then because it wasn't "as strong" of an urge. Ridiculous, I know. I continued to rationalize that maybe after a little longer delay, it would just go away completely. (I've told you before to use my life as your example of what *not* to do. You're welcome.)

It took a while and a few reminders on God's part before I finally gave in. But in His gentle reminders, I realized my delayed obedience was disobedience—. and because I disobeyed, there would be a cost—one, I might never fully realize. Had I acted yesterday when I felt strongly about it, who knows what God was prepared to do? Had I acted yesterday, maybe the timing would've been ideal, but my disobedience might have cost God being able to use or bless my act the way He had planned. Ultimately, I'll never know. But what I *do* know is this: Even though I obeyed God today, it doesn't change the fact I disobeyed Him yesterday. It also doesn't change what it reveals about my heart and my attitude toward God.

My disobedience shows I care more about what I think someone might think about me than what God thinks. It reveals that while He's important; He's not *more* important than I am. It reveals that while I seek God's will and direction; I'm hesitant to obey Him if I don't agree or understand why I need to. My delay shows I still have much work to do in submitting myself to God and being willing to be humble before Him and others.

In this season of your life, is there something God's been asking you to do that you keep delaying? Is there something that, due to your perception of what others may think, you haven't obeyed Him fully? Is there something that might seem small to you, and maybe you've decided to obey—eventually—but haven't yet? Whatever reasoning you're using to not obey God immediately, I mean *right now,* check the source of that "reasoning." Could it be your delayed obedience is costing you countless blessings—maybe even the very ones you've been praying for? If there is something, please learn from me, and don't delay. Just obey.

Rooting Ourselves in Christ

Is there something God has asked you to do that you have delayed in your obedience? What is keeping you from obeying God today?

_____

_____

_____

_____

_____

_____

_____

_____

_____

_____

Day Fifty-Two
Justified

We are continuing to monitor Chris's low-grade fever and increased liver enzymes. There are still lots of unknowns in a situation that can change at any time, but we remain hopeful that the enzyme increase is due to medication and the stent he received a month ago and, in time, will resolve on its own without surgical intervention.

The kids and I were enjoying a rare cool summer morning. As I watched the kids playing, I saw my oldest retaliate against his younger sister because of a hurt she had inflicted on him minutes before. Being the designated peacemaker, I called my son over to talk about his choices, and that's when I heard God speak to me through the words I was saying to my son.

As his mom, I spoke about how he retaliated because his sister had hurt him (intentionally or not), and he had yet to forgive her (regardless of whether she had apologized or asked for forgiveness). I explained how he was allowing his hurt to build a wall between himself and his sister. I asked him who wants that wall there. Who wants him to focus on his hurt feelings and demand an apology before forgiving her? God or the Enemy?

As I had that conversation with my son, I very clearly understood the same applied to me. As adults, our hurts may seem bigger or feel deeper than those of a child. But ultimately, a hurt is a hurt and *all* must be addressed. Each hurt inflicted or received becomes a choice. My heart, once injured, doesn't want to forgive. My heart demands a penance to be paid. It demands justice.

When you've been hurt, it's easy to justify almost any response to the one who inflicted the pain. It's easy to withhold forgiveness that hasn't been "earned" or asked for. Regardless of how justified we might be, God calls each of us to respond differently. He calls us to respond like Christ.

As Christians, we are called to do the hard work and respond *beyond* our feelings, forgiving even when we don't want to—even when we still feel the sting of the hurt. Jesus directly addresses this with Peter in Matthew 18:21-22:

> "Then Peter came and said to Him, "Lord, how often shall my brother sin against me and I forgive him? Up to seven times?" Jesus said to him, "I do not say to you, up to seven times, but up to seventy times seven."

Over and over in the Bible, God teaches us that *love* bears all things and does not consider a wrong suffered (1 Corinthians 13:5). While it isn't always easy and often takes intentional time to work through, it is so important to forgive and not allow the Enemy build walls of unforgiveness that will separate you from others.

The very words I spoke to my son, God was speaking to me.

If you've been carrying a hurt, lay it down and forgive the person. Do it over and over and over, if necessary, until you can easily ask God to bless them. Your forgiveness doesn't excuse the action or ask that you forget what happened. Forgiveness doesn't require you to make future choices that will allow you to be hurt again. But it *is* about letting go of the pain and the anger and giving it to God. It's about realizing *every* hurtful thing *you* have done (intentional or not) and understanding that you, too, desire others to forgive you. It's realizing that God has forgiven us far more than anything we will ever be asked to forgive from others. Forgiveness is about refusing to allow the Enemy to build another wall to separate you from others or God. It's about remembering the hurt you feel just enough to consistently ask for forgiveness and admit your mistakes the moment you are aware of them. It's learning to ask for forgiveness from others the way you wish it would've been asked from you.

We are all flawed human beings stumbling through this dark place we call life. Be a light that others can follow. Tear down the walls that are keeping you apart. Justified or not, forgive anyway.

Rooting Ourselves in Christ

What hurt are you carrying that you need to lay down and forgive?

_____

_____

_____

_____

_____

_____

_____

_____

_____

_____

_____

Day Fifty-Three
Dangers of Distraction

The physical difficulties of so much still unhealed are one thing, but over the next seven days Chris will spend Father's Day, our daughter's 4th birthday, and our 18th wedding anniversary all in the hospital. I cannot fathom how lonely this must feel for him trapped in a body that doesn't move and can't speak. Please pray for his healing—physical, mental, emotional—as well as the kids; this week.

In our 150+ day journey, I can tell you story after story about how I've felt God talk to me. Driving to and from the hospital, I might hear a message I knew was just for me. Reading a passage in the Bible might lead to something jumping off the page that I hadn't noticed before and feeling like it was intended just for me. This week, I realized I have spent so much of my time being focused on various projects and tasks that I haven't heard that special message yet. I haven't felt inspired to pour out whatever God was showing me onto paper. As I looked up and realized how "quiet" God has seemed, it occurred to me that I have been too busy, too distracted, and I haven't stopped long enough for God to speak. Even when I'm not moving from place to place, my mind is.

I find myself wondering now, as I write this, just how much *have* I missed from God? How many words of wisdom, encouragement, and inspiration did He have ready to give me, but I haven't been still or quiet enough to receive them? How many times did I make things more difficult than they had to be because I haven't spent time with God? How many times have I not slept well or been unnecessarily upset because I didn't start my day with the Author of *love, peace, and hope*?

Psalms 1:1-3 says:

> "Blessed is the one who does not walk in step with the wicked or stand in the way that sinners take or sit in the company of mockers, but whose delight is in the law of the Lord, and who meditates on his law day and night. That person is like a tree planted by streams of water, which yields its fruit in season and whose leaf does not wither—whatever they do prospers."

I don't want to walk through a single season that doesn't yield fruit. I want to perpetually have "leaves" so well nourished they never wither. I want whatever I do to prosper. It's a wonderful sentiment. But, to receive the blessings found in Psalm 1:3— a prosperous life that yields fruit—I *must first* do what Psalms 1:1-2 says. My prosperous life and fruit are directly tied to my daily decision to live a life that delights in the law and meditates on God's word day and night.

It's easy to skim past the first two verses and wonder why our lives don't seem more prosperous. If my daily decisions don't involve spending time with God, learning his word, and studying what He teaches regarding my heart and attitudes, then I *won't* live a life with leaves that don't wither when times are hard.

The last few weeks have been especially difficult, personally, and I've often wondered why things must be harder than they should be. Over the last few weeks, it's been easy to blame or rationalize or explain why things are difficult, but ultimately, it comes down to my choices regarding my time. I've been distracted. I've been "lazy." I've reasoned I needed a break.

When I consider how I spend my time and the choices I make, I realize they've been neither helpful to me nor God-seeking. My food choices don't serve my body and my chronic illness well. My time choices don't support trying to launch one business and revamp another well. My sleep choices (or lack thereof) don't benefit this stressful season. Over and over the past few weeks, I've "planned" to spend time with God, and then I got distracted or side-tracked and didn't.

And I wonder why it's been hard. I wonder why I don't feel strong. Why I feel on edge. Why I don't have peace. If I don't *begin* my day with the one who *is* peace, then how long do I really think I can maintain it without Him?

Life is hard—for all of us. Life gets busy, and we get easily distracted. Spending time with God, daily, needs to be as nonnegotiable as brushing our teeth or washing our hands. The Enemy will do whatever he can to distract or dissuade us to put off our time with God. He'll get us to do to ourselves what he does not have permission to do to us.

If it's been awhile since you've spent some one-on-one time with God, stop right now and do just that. It doesn't have to be hours, but it does have to be consistent. Find a verse or use this verse from Psalms and meditate on it throughout the day. Ask God to show you where in your day you can spend more time with Him. Ask Him what schedule changes you need to make to make room for Him. Ultimately if we want to live a life that yields fruit, then our lives *must* remain grafted to His.

Rooting Ourselves in Christ

How has life distracted you from walking more closely with God?

_____

_____

_____

_____

_____

_____

Day Fifty-Four
Feelings

Chris has had a rough few days as he developed another low-grade fever and his heartrate climbed fairly high. Unfortunately, he has remained tachycardic since. We've begun more medications to help lower his heart rate while monitoring his already low blood pressure. It continues to be a balancing act of fixing one thing without breaking another.

Feelings. We all have them. While some are unspeakably strong and pull us down paths we wouldn't have willingly chosen, others are fleeting and fickle—changing more often than we change our clothes. As I stop and examine my daily choices, it's shocking how much weight I have given these finicky emotions.

More than I want to admit, I tend to eat healthy "when I feel like it." I work out or wake up early to have quiet time with God usually "when I feel like it." I model patience and grace with my kids or others when "I'm in a good mood," and I model impatience and short-temperedness when I'm not. As I was reading 1 John 2:1-6 this morning, I realized that I have allowed my feelings to rule my actions and emotions for far too long.

1 John 2:1 begins by saying,

"My dear children, I write this to you so that you will not sin."

It only took me a few verses to realize that *because* I have allowed my emotions to reign unchecked and control the actions in my life, I have "sinned." Throughout the Bible, God reminds us that we *will* feel strong emotions like anger, but *when* we do, to not sin—to not let our emotions dictate our attitudes and responses. (See Ephesians 4:26.)

While there's a lot to unpack between verse 1 and verse 6, it was verse 6 that really got my attention.

1 John 2:6 reads,

"Whoever claims to live in Him must live as Jesus did."

What hit me is that we are to *live* and *act* as Jesus did. It's when we don't act as Jesus did that we tend to "sin." This verse made me pause and realize that the Bible doesn't focus on Jesus's feelings about things, but rather His actions *despite* His feelings. Occasionally, we read that Jesus wept or was angry, but even in these moments, Jesus's choices actions were never based on how He felt. I'm sure that Jesus must have felt exhausted throughout His ministry. But even after preaching all day, He was never short-tempered with His disciples, and He *always* showed them love, grace, and patience—especially when they didn't understand Him. Being human, Jesus's feelings were hurt from time to time, but He still acted lovingly and graciously toward people who harmed Him. Jesus did not allow His feelings to control His behavior.

Conviction swept over me when I paused and considered how well I was doing living like Jesus did. Sure, I have moments when I'm patient and loving and gentle to my children or others who may frustrate me or hurt my feelings. But often, my actions speak *much louder* than my words—or who I claim lives in my heart.

As a wife, mom, entrepreneur, and current single parent and sole bread winner, there's *a lot* on my plate. It would be "understandable" or "excusable" to snap at those around me and be short-tempered with those who annoy me. But, is that what Jesus did? Is that how *He* lived His life? If I want my life to reflect the difference He's made in it, then my actions—every day—must reflect His. As I contemplated this verse, I realized people will watch me for signs of Jesus—especially when I've been hurt. Even though I profess to walk *with* God, if my actions and choices don't reflect that—*especially* when it's the hardest—then how many times have I missed being the light that directs others back to Him?

How many people have taken my poor choices and emotional decisions as evidence that they don't need God? How many times has my sin of unchecked, emotionally based actions been a stumbling block to their faith?

Over the past several months, I've watched as my oldest child mirrors me more than I'd like. It's not my great qualities or characteristics that I see being reflected; it's my bad attitudes and impatience. I've watched him repeatedly treat his sister in ways that hurt my heart, and I realize it's a direct reflection of how I've treated them or someone else.

What then, as Christians, are we to do? How can we make different choices?

For me, there are three things I'm focusing on. First, I must spend *daily* time with God. How will I ever see an action as the sin it is, and understand my need to change, if I don't have daily check-ins with my Savior? Second, I need to be genuinely repentant for my choices, actions, and attitudes. I must ask forgiveness from God and others when I have sinned against them. Humbling ourselves to others is a hard, but necessary step. Third, I must use my God-given stubbornness for good and set my mind that I will *act* loving and patient and grace-filled until my feelings catch up. Regardless of how I *feel*, I must still choose to act as Jesus would—to ask myself over and over and over, if necessary, the old WWJD (What would Jesus do?) question. If Jesus were in my place, how would *He* respond? How would *he* treat this person? Are my *actions* (not my feelings) mirroring His?

I encourage you to take your own personal inventory. If you've been hurt, frustrated, annoyed, or disappointed, do your actions reflect your *feelings* rather than *God*? If so, pray first. Ask for forgiveness, and admit you've been wrong. Then, choose to *act* like Jesus until your feelings catch up! Eventually, they will.

Rooting Ourselves in Christ

How can you act as Jesus would despite your feelings? Where are you struggling the most? Ask God for the strength to 'act' the way Jesus did regardless of how you feel.

_____

_____

_____

_____

_____

_____

_____

_____

_____

_____

Day Fifty-Five
Stewardship

*I am writing this update from the waiting room of
Interventional Radiology (IR). It's clear I've been here
too much: the EMTs knew my name, and the staff saw
me coming, came over for hugs, and put me to work.
We're relocating the initial pancreatic drain and adding
a secondary drain into a separate pancreatic fluid
pocket. Next, we'll aspirate and culture the fluid in his
lungs. His WBC has continued to climb slowly with no
clear cause. He continues to run a low-grade fever and
becomes tachycardic quickly without medicine to bring
his heart rate down.*

Matthew 25:14-30 tells the parable of the talents. In
this account, we find a wealthy man who leaves town
and entrusts talents to his servants. (A talent was a sum
of money worth about 20 years of a servant's wages.)
To one, he gives five talents, to another two talents,
and to a third servant he gives just one. While some
servants were offered many talents, everyone was
given at least one.

We, as Christians, are no different. Some of us may
have giftings to do many things, and some of us may
have talents to do a few things. But *all* of us have been
entrusted with *something* by our master. God is
entrusting us to steward well what He has given us.

Unfortunately, we often miss God's plan of stewardship because we assume it applies solely to our money. But God wants us to steward well so much more. He's given each of us certain talents and abilities to use to draw others to Him. God *gave* them to us for the sole purpose of penetrating the world and growing more believers—the multiplication effect. We were not given gifts and talents to make money, although that can be a side benefit. We were not given gifts and talents to make us happy, although this can be a perk. We were given them, so we can <u>use</u> them to reach others for Christ.

How many of us are actively, daily looking for ways to do that? Sometimes we mistakenly think that only paid ministers are designed or called to do this, but we are *all* are called. You may think your world is limited to your home, your neighborhood, and your workplace. However, in today's growing age of technology, where we're all just a few clicks away from being connected, your world is so much bigger. What are you doing to reach others through your Facebook posts or Twitter feeds? Are you concerned with keeping up appearances and making sure others know how #blessed you are, or are you busy trying to use the gifts God gave you for His glory?

To use your gifts, you must *know* them. Do you? When was the last time you not only spent time understanding what your gifts are, but also reflecting on how to better incorporate them into your life and how you spend your time? Are you too busy doing "stuff" that you don't have room to prioritize your time effectively and grow the gifts He's entrusted to you?

Maybe you have the Enemy's voice inside your head, spewing lies and trying to convince you your talents aren't special and there's nothing truly unique about you. Mistakenly, you've believed these lies and never pushed yourself to further develop your special gifts. Maybe you believed that if it's hard, it must not be where God wants you. That if you're rowing against the wind, you must be in the wrong place or doing the wrong thing. God placed you in this spot to row against the wind, so you will *know* it's *God* and not *you* that made it possible. He *wants* you to struggle so you *need* Him. He knows if it's not a struggle, you'll mistakenly believe you did it on your own.

The Enemy tells you that if it's hard, it's not of God because he wants you to get stuck. He wants you to be immobile—not moving, not growing, not helping anyone. He lies, hoping you'll keep your gifts and talents buried so they're not producing fruit—not in your life or in anyone else's.

Knowing your spiritual gifts, talents, and strengths isn't something that's nice to do or great for others; it's essential for *you* if you're going to yield the fruit in your life that God has planned. I passionately believe that to be fully rooted in Christ, we must know our intrinsic uniqueness. And, if I'm being honest, I have struggled with this very thing for a long time.

For more years than I care to admit, I believed the Enemy's lie. I believed I'm not enough—not good enough, smart enough, pretty enough, talented enough, fill-in-the-blank enough. But all of these "not enough" are based on lies, not on who God says I am.

They're not based on God's opinion of me. They're not based how He sees me as His daughter whom He dearly loves—a daughter He longs will *finally* use her gifts and talents for her Father's glory. God knows the abilities within me, and He wants me to see them, believe in them, and use them to help others find their way to Him. He knows my life can have an impact on others—not because *I'm* special, but because *He* is. He desperately wants me to know and believe that, too.

Rooting Ourselves in Christ

Spend some time over the next few weeks really examining your life. Do you know your spiritual gifts, talents, strengths? Are you actively developing them and using them? Are you using them to be a light for God in this dark world? God handpicked each of those gifts for you. He personally put together each aspect of your personality because He knows you can impact your world for His glory. He desperately wants you to see yourself and your abilities the way He does. Steward your gifts well. Let them multiply for His glory and your deep gladness.

_____

_____

Day Fifty-Six
Rowing Against the Wind

Chris continues to have an elevated WBC and low-grade fever. We've taken additional cultures as we search for a cause. The results we have so far show new infections in both his lungs and pancreatic fluid.

I had the privilege of speaking to the faculty and staff at my children's school a few weeks ago. In my remarks to them, I included a section of dreams I have for my kids. It wasn't until after my talk that I realized just how powerful these dreams are for me, too. In my list, I included:

- *To realize "hard" is not bad, rather it's an opportunity for growth.*
- *To appreciate anyone can do "easy," which is why easy has little value.*
- *To understand that anything of value in life— any dream you have for yourself—will be filled with hard work, hard days, and hard times. Knowing how to push through and past the hard now will prepare you to be successful later.*
- *To find one thing each month you didn't think you could do and do it. And if you fail, to keep trying until you succeed—because eventually, you will.*

- *To know all great leaders were failures first, and to not be afraid to follow in their footsteps.*

I was struck by a realization about how I handle "hard things." When things become especially difficult, I ascribe certain beliefs that may not necessarily be true. Until recently, I have always mistakenly assumed having the wind against me was a sign I was rowing in the wrong direction. For most of my life, I assumed that if I was where God wanted me to be, doing the things He sent me to do, life would be easy. I should have His hand and grace and blessings on me. Where I came up with these misguided beliefs, I have no idea.

In God's infinite wisdom, He perfectly timed a message from Steven Furtick titled, "It's Often Hard to See the Significance in Your Season." As I listened to his message, I was awestruck by his words.

In his message, Steven focuses on Mark 6:45-52. This passage begins right after Jesus has miraculously fed 5000 people with a little boy's lunch. After Jesus performs this miracle and 12 baskets of leftovers are gathered and placed in the disciples' boat, Mark 6:45 states,

> "Immediately Jesus made his disciples get into the boat and go on ahead of him to Bethsaida, while he dismissed the crowd."

Did you catch that? Omniscient Jesus *sends* His disciples into the boat to go ahead of Him to Bethsaida. Then a few verses later we read,

> "He saw the disciples straining at the oars, because the wind was against them."

While Steven goes on to make lots of impactful points, I wanted to focus on one. In this passage, the disciples were obediently going exactly where Jesus sent them, in the exact manner He had asked them to travel. There wasn't delayed obedience; the disciples had done the very thing Jesus had commanded. And yet, "they were straining at the oars because the wind was against them." When Jesus sent them, He *knew* they would be rowing into a storm, and He sent them anyway. In fact, it was hours later, shortly before dawn, before Jesus came to them.

I was so surprised by the realization that God often sends us places where He knows we'll be rowing into the wind. He sends us places He knows will require His ability to calm the winds for us to have safe passage. Countless times in my life, I've sought God's guidance and direction and wrongly assumed when things seemed too strenuous that I must have heard wrong. Instead, God may have sent me to row against the wind *so that* I would learn to depend on Him and not on my own abilities. He may have sent me *so that* when things calmed, I would know it was Jesus who calmed them and not me. In verse 51 we read,

> "Then he climbed into the boat with them, and the wind died down."

It wasn't until Jesus climbed into the boat with the disciples that the winds finally calmed. How often have I needed God to do just that but never rowed long enough to give Him the opportunity? How many times have I taken a storm as a "sign" and headed for shore—completely disobeying what I clearly heard God tell me to do, simply because it became difficult? How many times have I missed experiencing His power and authority over my situation because I didn't trust Him to come to me and climb into my storm with me?

If God has called you to go somewhere or do something, don't give up just because it's hard. Lean into the wind and keep rowing until He calms your storm. Trust that God knows the difficulties you are rowing against and that He has allowed it for a reason and for a season. Trust that He sees you in the storm. At no point were the disciples out of Jesus's line of sight even while He prayed. Keep rowing. Keep obeying. Keep waiting for Jesus to climb into your boat. He's walking out to meet you right where you are.

Rooting Ourselves in Christ

Ask God to show you tangible examples of how you remain in His sight. Where have you seen God in the boat with you during this storm?

_____

_____

Day Fifty-Seven
Judging the Rich, Young Ruler

Chris has officially passed the 90-day window of acute kidney injury and has transitioned to chronic kidney failure or end-stage renal disease. With new pancreatic and lung infections, he'll likely be on new medicines through the end of the year. He will be having his fourth ERCP soon. We're hopeful we can finally remove the stones in his common bile duct. Chris still has a long and arduous journey ahead.

I'm judgmental; I admit it. I wish I weren't, and I try not to be, but I am. I wrongly judge other people and place them on my scale of "appropriateness" based on my own life experiences, thoughts, and beliefs. Sadly, my judging doesn't stop there. I judge the people of the Bible and the choices they make just as harshly. In my misplaced superiority, I have, for years, read the story of the "rich, young ruler" and thrown stones at this poor man— never once realizing it's a story about my own heart.

Here's a brief recap in case it's been awhile. We find this story in Mark 10:17-27. It begins when a man asks Jesus what he needed to do to "inherit eternal life." Jesus tells the man he must keep the commandments:

"Do not murder. Do not commit adultery. Do not steal. Do not bear false witness. Do not defraud. Honor your father and mother."

The rich, young ruler replies in verse 20:
"Teacher, I have kept all these things from my youth up."

Then Jesus lovingly looked at him and said in verse 21:
"One thing you lack, go, sell everything you have and give to the poor, and you will have treasure in heaven. Then come, follow me."

[22] "At this the man's face fell. He went away sad, because he had great wealth."

It's important to not dismiss the man's response so quickly. He very clearly states that he knows the commandments and has been following God's law since he was young. To be this obedient requires a good amount of effort and shows that living a godly life was important to him. It was likely something he had prayed about consistently. (As the daughter of a Southern Baptist Minister, I can relate to being aware of God's commandments since my youth and trying to uphold them.)

Jesus knew that even though following God's law was important to this young man, it wasn't more important than his financial security. It's easy to judge this if it isn't our issue. *But we all have a stronghold.* Maybe it's unforgiveness, maybe it's submission, maybe it's respectfulness, maybe it is financial security. How often have we prayed for something we want God to change, but in the same breath refuse to do the one thing He's asking us to do? To forgive and treat lovingly the person who deeply hurt us. To submit to our boss or our spouse when we don't think they deserve it, or we believe they are clearly wrong. Maybe it's treating respectfully our children or our neighbor or that one coworker or family member whom we don't like. Maybe it's giving our money to God and trusting Him to provide.

It's easy to judge someone who is struggling with an issue we're not. What's *not* easy, is when you realize you're just as guilty, maybe even more, within your own area of struggle. If it were easy to follow Christ, then we'd all do it. But we don't. We sit back and check our Sunday morning church attendance box and think giving my entire life over to God is great for *that* person, but God doesn't understand...*what*? Doesn't understand your responsibilities? Your hurt? Your pain? Your struggles? What exactly do you think God doesn't understand about your life?

The rich young ruler wanted eternal life, but he wanted financial comfort and security in this life even more. What are you asking God for—and what have you been unwilling to give up to receive it? Are you asking for a better marriage, but you're not willing to treat your spouse with love and honor regardless of how they treat you? Are you asking for a better job and financial security, but you're not willing to tithe and help others with the finances you have now?

Whatever your struggle, I hope you'll learn from the rich young ruler and realize Jesus is looking lovingly at you, wanting you to realize how much more you will gain if you'll simply lay down your stronghold, too.

Rooting Ourselves in Christ

The rich, young ruler struggled with selling all his worldly possessions to follow Christ. Where do you struggle? How could God use this storm to help you trust Him more than the area of your stronghold?

_____

_____

_____

_____

_____

_____

_____

_____

Day Fifty-Eight
You Are Valuable

I'm hopeful that MAYBE we can finally get the stones removed from Chris's common bile duct during the upcoming ERCP. Overall, not a lot has changed. His liver enzymes are still significantly elevated, but his WBC count is trending down, and he hasn't had fever in a week.

You, my friend, are valuable. I know you want to argue that statement and say, "If only you knew me better, you'd think differently." You want to tell me all the reasons you are not. If you could, you might share the dark secrets that prove you're anything *but* valuable. Maybe you make choices because you believe your life has little real value to anyone—so you drink more than you should, you smoke, you binge eat, you've developed addictions you wish you could stop. Maybe you're disgusted by your reflection in the mirror.

I know.

But, right now, right where you are, *you are valuable.*

Your value isn't dependent on your parents who hurt you when you were young. Your value isn't tied to your net worth or the size of your house or the car you drive. Your value isn't how your spouse makes you feel or doesn't. It isn't connected to your ability to have kids or find a significant other in life. Your value isn't related to the choices you made in college and now try to hide. Your value is so much more.

How do I know you're valuable? I know because Jesus came to die for you. But I know you wonder if you're experiencing a storm because Jesus has forgotten and abandoned you. In your storm, you believe God must be punishing you because you deserve it. You feel forgotten, unseen, and alone. You believe the lie that if you mattered, truly mattered, things would be different. Things would be better.

Sweet friend, if I could, I'd meet you for coffee and listen to you as you recount every wrong choice made, every fact about your life that "proves" you are not valuable, and then I'd give you a hug and a squeeze of the hand and share Jesus with you.

Jesus came for *you*. He sought *you*. He loves *you*—not the perfect you or the filtered you, but the real you. The one no one else knows. He sees and hears your cries. He desperately wants you to see and know just how valuable and special you are.

Little by little, the Enemy has whispered his lies to you. Maybe they started when you were young, and you assumed those thoughts must be the truth. But you hear them now louder than ever. Lies that blame and discourage your heart. Lies that try to demonstrate misplaced value on the wrong things or encourage you to numb the hurt through choices that will ultimately bring you death. Those choices have been easy for you to make, because why would you want to choose differently if your life isn't worth anything? The Enemy has helped you build wall after wall to separate you from the people who care most about you. He's told you they're only here to remind you that you're not good enough.

My sweet friend, my heart breaks for you and with you. While I'd love to share reason after reason why you're valuable to God, I'm going to share just one, probably unusual, story.

Mark 4:35-5:20 tells a story about Jesus driving out an army of demons from a man. The man had been possessed by the demons for a very long time. When Jesus decides to cross the lake "to the other side to the region of the Gerasenes" where the demon-possessed man was living among the tombs, a fierce storm developed. Mark 4:37 says:

> "A furious squall came up, and the waves broke over the boat, so that it was nearly swamped."

I wonder just how many furious squalls you're facing? How many waves are breaking over your boat so that you fear it will go under? The storms in this passage arose to prevent Jesus from reaching the demon-possessed man, we read in Mark 4:39:

> "He [Jesus] got up, rebuked the wind and said to the waves, 'Quiet! Be still!' Then the wind died down and it was completely calm."

No one who lives near this demon-possessed man believed he is of any value. No one cared about him. This man is unseen and forgotten and lived among the dead.

> Mark 5:5: "Night and day among the tombs and in the hills he would cry out and cut himself with stones."

Yet, Jesus, from a distance across a large lake, stops ministering and preaching to the throngs of people with Him and tends to this "unworthy" man. In Mark 5, Jesus drives out the "legion" of spirits who had been torturing this man for years.

Sweet friend, you too have spirits torturing you. No, they're not quite like this story, but you have allowed the Enemy to whisper lies for so long that you believe them and assume they are true. The Enemy has tortured you for so long, that you, too, are living a life among dead things.

Do you think the Enemy would go to this much trouble—sending a "furious squall" meant to capsize the boat Jesus is in and sending a legion of demons—if this man wasn't valuable to God? If he didn't have the capacity to impact countless lives for God, then why would the Enemy go to this great length to hurt him?

If your life doesn't have the capacity to impact countless lives for God and His kingdom, why is the Enemy spending so much time and effort to keep you believing his lies? Would *you* try and protect something that isn't *valuable*?

Pray. Ask God to rebuke all the lies you've mistakenly believed so you can begin to see yourself the way He does. Then read:

- Psalm 139:13-16
- Ephesians 2:4-9
- Jeremiah 29:11
- Luke 12:6-7
- Romans 5:8
- John 3:16

You *are valuable*, and God has mighty plans for your life! This story concludes with:

> "...the man went away and began to tell in the Decapolis[b] how much Jesus had done for him. And all the people were amazed."

Rooting Ourselves in Christ

How will your story end?

_____

_____

_____

_____

Day Fifty-Nine
Why Am I Valuable?

Chris has remained fever free and his liver enzymes have come down some. He's had a solid few days CPAPing when we've been able to reduce the positive pressure support a little. If this trend continues, it's possible sometime next week we might be able to try trach collaring again—which means maybe trying his speaking valve again.

As vital as it is to let your value to God take root in your heart, it's equally imperative for you to understand *why* you're so important to God. Yes, God is love, and He sacrificed Himself for you. Yes, you are made in the image of God. Yes, God sent His son to save you. But why? What did He save you *for*?

Is only your salvation the end goal? Or did God go through all of this for more? Does God want more for you and your life—*right now* and not just after you die? God left the splendors of heaven because He couldn't imagine being separated from you, but why is *your* life valuable to God?

I think many of us stay so focused on our own life and our own walk that we never look up and look beyond ourselves. God hand-picked every detail about you for a reason. He wanted you to grow up exactly when and where you did *for a reason*. He wanted you to have the parents you had and life experiences you had for a reason. Is it possible that God has been waiting for you to realize your value and the calling He placed on your life so that you can reach another?

Jesus gives the "great commission" in Mark 16:15:

> "And he said to them, 'Go into all the world and preach and publish openly the good news (the Gospel) to every creature.'"

Did you just assume that Jesus was only talking to the disciples? Maybe you thought He meant preachers or missionaries? Jesus meant *you*. He called *you* to go into *your* world and lead others back to Him.

You're valuable because someone is waiting for you to share Jesus with them. Before you were even created, God planned that your life, your walk, your calling would help lead people back to Him—people with whom you would uniquely interact. He planned your life so you would plant another seed for His kingdom. *That* is why keeping you from your calling is so important to the Enemy.

The Enemy is willing to do *whatever* it takes to keep you distracted, discouraged, busy, or downtrodden. He wants you out of your calling and away from the people in your world you're meant to reach.

John 10:10 reminds us:

> "The thief comes only to steal and kill and destroy; I [Jesus] have come that they may have life and have it to the full."

It's the Enemy's job to steal whatever is valuable. That, my friend, is *you* and *your calling*. He will lie, cheat, steal, kill, and destroy whatever he can to keep you feeling stuck, trapped, and useless. Your influence on another life is invaluable in the kingdom. But there is a catch.

God's plans will be accomplished with or without your help. Mordecai gives us a great reminder of that in Esther 4:14:

> "For if you remain silent at this time, relief and deliverance for the Jews will arise from another place, but you and your father's family will perish. And who knows but that you have come to your royal position for such a time as this?"

I wonder how many blessings we have missed because we haven't moved beyond our own "salvation" to seeking a life of purpose?

Rooting Ourselves in Christ

What do you think God saved you for? What role do you have to play in His kingdom work?

_____

_____

_____

_____

_____

_____

_____

_____

_____

_____

_____

_____

_____

_____

Day Sixty
My Problem with Prayer

Chris continues to remain in constant pain and severe nausea. We've added even more medicines to help keep him comfortable, but the realization that the more we diminish his pain, the more we diminish his GI tract's ability to work—which impacts his nausea and the high NG output as well as other organs we're desperately trying to repair. It is impossible to address any one issue without it having an overlapping impact on another area.

Over the past 180 days, I've prayed a lot. I tend to spend my prayer time telling God, reminding God, asking God, pleading with God my needs and desires. Whether I have five minutes or 25 minutes, my prayer time has been about *me*. Over and over, I have failed to remember that God knows my needs and desires; He doesn't need me to remind Him. Sometimes, at the end of my prayer time I feel better for having voiced my concerns out loud. Other times, as the "amen" leaves my lips, I still feel anxious and worried and wonder why my prayers don't seem to help.

Recently, as I listened to a pastor speak about the power of prayer and how prayer is different from simply *talking* about a problem, I realized what I was missing.

Sure, I was checking my box on "praying," but I was only talking about my problems to God. I should have been telling my problems who my God is. Praying gives me an opportunity to worship and recall all of God's names and His nature. Prayer reminds me that He is sovereign over ALL my needs. As I pray, peace, blessings, and power   come as I focus on how great and mighty God is.

I took the pastor's advice and began to write out the various names and nature of God. Below is a small sample.

- El Shaddai-The Lord God Almighty
- Jehovah Raah-The Lord My Shepherd
- Jehovah Rapha-The Lord who Heals
- Jehovah Shammah-The Lord is There
- El Olam-The Everlasting God
- Jehovah Jireh-The Lord Will Provide
- El Roi-The God Who Sees
- Jehovah Mekoddishkem-The Lord Who Sanctifies
- Jehovah Nissi-The Lord is My Victory
- Jehovah Shalom-The Lord is Peace
- Jehovah Adon Kal Ha'arets-The Lord of All the Earth
- Jehovah Gibbor Milchamah-The Lord is Mighty in Battle
- Jehovah Go'el-The Redeemer
- Jehovah Hoshe'ah-The Lord Who Saves
- Jehovah Machsi-The Lord is My Refuge
- Jehovah Uzi-The Lord My Strength

Instead of telling God what He already knows regarding my needs, I am focused on reminding myself and my problems who my God is. He is Jehovah Jireh who provides all that I need. He is Jehovah Uzi, my strength. No matter what I'm walking through, God is El Roi and Jehovah Machsi—the One who Sees and my Refuge. As I walk through storm after storm, I have Jehovah Shammah and Jehovah Gibbor Milchamah—the God who is There and the God who is Mighty in Battle—walking *in* my storm with me. On the days I worry whether Chris's body will heal, I remind myself that my God is Jehovah Rapha—the Lord who Heals.

Whatever you're facing, whatever storm you're walking through, seek God's name in it and pray that over and over. Watch and see how His spirit will flood you as you pray. God is your Provider, your Redeemer, your Refuge. Worship Him, not your problems.

Rooting Ourselves in Christ

Which of God's names speaks peace, strength, hope to you in this storm?

_____

_____

Day Sixty-One
Is God Enough?

It's officially day 207. Chris is back in the STICU a little longer after another spike in his fever. We're culturing everything again and looking for a cause we can address. We're disappointed in the lack of success from his 5th ERCP attempt, as well as discouraged by Chris's increased illnesses as he has developed another lung infection after his lungs were seeing so much improvement last week.

I often hear Christians (myself included) quote Ephesians 3:20:

> "Now to Him who is able to do infinitely more than all we ask or imagine, according to His power that is at work within us."

It's a great verse of encouragement when I'm walking through a stormy season. During these hard times, I find it's easy to focus on the *bigness* of God. God is big enough to heal Chris. He's big enough to provide for our family and to give us the wisdom we desperately need. God is big enough to open doors for us and big enough to provide peace which passes all understanding. He's big enough for miracles and big enough to make the impossible possible. Over and over I pray about needing

God's "bigness" and often share with others just how big He really is. While I don't always know if, when, or how God will choose to answer one of my many prayers, I rarely question His "bigness."

As I drove to the hospital this morning, I realized that most of my relationship with God is centered on my ever-growing list of needs, not on Him. I realized that I'm seeking Him to meet my needs, rather than seeking Him— the "Meeter" of those needs. If God chose to not answer any more prayers, would He still be enough for me?

Am I seeking what I *want* from God more than I'm seeking *God*?

If God chose to never heal Chris—if Chris is as healthy today as he'll ever be—would I *still* pray and praise God? If God chose to neither provide for our family nor open any doors for us, would I *still* seek Him? If God chose to not bless us with anything else until the day we join Him in heaven, is He enough? Has what He has *already* done through the shedding of His blood for my sins enough for me?

I began to wonder if my relationship with God is more about what I think God will someday *do for me* rather than knowing and worshipping Him. Do I spend time with God to keep my proverbial foot in the door with Him? Or am I spending time with Him because I want to get to know Him better?

This realization hit me hard. The raw truth usually does. While I'd like to think God saving me from my sins is enough, my actions don't reflect that. My prayers and pleadings are, at their core, about what I think God will do for me.

The truth is, I spend very little time trying to know more about His nature simply because I value Him. The time I spend studying His word is for my benefit, not to draw closer to Him.

I have so much heart work still to do. I want to seek God and draw closer to Him because of who He is, not because of what He can do for me. I want God to be enough—even if our lives never change or improve. I want to have joy and peace in who God is, not in what He has done for me.

Rooting Ourselves in Christ

Before your next quiet time, examine how you're spending your time with God. If God never answers your requests and never blesses you with anything more than what you have today, is that enough? Is He enough for you? Are you seeking Him because you want your prayers answered or are you simply seeking God to know Him more completely? If your storm never improves or changes, is God still enough? This continues to be a difficult question for me to honestly answer. My prayer is that even as you walk through this difficult season, you'll seek God MORE than you seek your desires.

_____

_____

_____

_____

_____

_____

_____

_____

_____

_____

_____

_____

_____

_____

Conclusion

As I finalize the components of this book, we have officially reached day 320. Just a few days ago, Chris was released from his long-term acute care facility and admitted to an inpatient rehabilitation hospital closer to home. While our storm continues, I pray that you have found encouragement and strength through each devotional which was written during this time. Our family has closed one chapter of fighting for Chris's survival and have begun another difficult chapter as we battle the painful and often microscopic steps towards healing and recovery. We have walked through almost every holiday including the start of a new calendar year as our family waits to be reunited under one roof. Even with all the uncertainty that continues to await us, I remain thankful for the redeeming love of God that is at work in our lives.

Through each storm you experience, remember there are spectators waiting and watching to see what you choose to do with the debris of your life once the rain and the winds have subsided. Do you praise God over the remnants left behind? Do you curse God for all that was lost? Do you spend your time helping your neighbor rebuild or focus solely on yourself?

As I reflect on my own missteps along the way, I've realized my greatest joy and my greatest peace came on the days when I began them intentionally rooted in Christ. The days where I could share God's light with another or help-even in very small ways-brought much needed joy and relief to my weary heart. I hope you can learn as I did and become rooted in Christ each day. I pray you will delight yourself in the Lord and live a life of encouragement, peace, and joy in Him—and that His light would shine through your darkness to others.

From one storm survivor to another...
Much love,

Beth

51033867R00124

Made in the USA
Columbia, SC
12 February 2019

Skyhorse Publishing books may be purchased in bulk at special discounts for sales promotion, corporate gifts, fund-raising, or educational purposes. Special editions can also be created to specifications. For details, contact the Special Sales Department, Skyhorse Publishing, 307 West 36th Street, 11th Floor, New York, NY 10018 or info@skyhorsepublishing.com.

Skyhorse® and Skyhorse Publishing® are registered trademarks of Skyhorse Publishing, Inc.®, a Delaware corporation.

Visit our website at www.skyhorsepublishing.com.

10 9 8 7 6 5 4 3 2 1

Library of Congress Cataloging-in-Publication Data is available on file.

Cover design by David Ter-Avanesyan

ISBN: 978-1-5107-8490-1
Ebook ISBN: 978-1-5107-8508-3

Printed in the United States of America

Can I Say That?

Why Free Speech Matters and How to Use It Fearlessly

Dr. Chloe Carmichael

Skyhorse Publishing